MEDIEVAL CRAFTSMEN
GOLDSMITHS
JOHN CHERRY

BRITISH MUSEUM PRESS

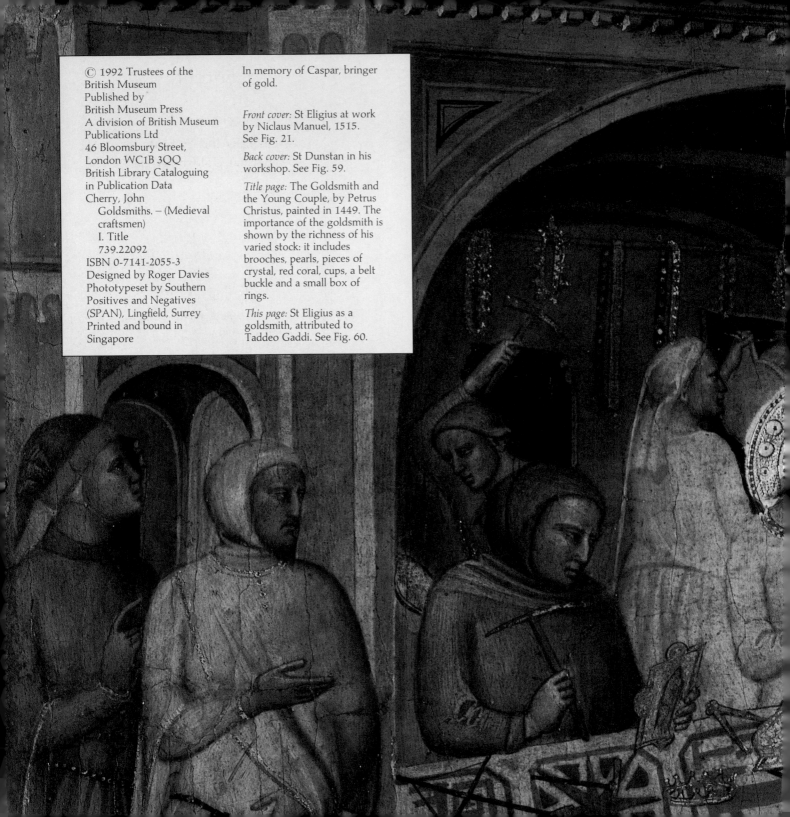

© 1992 Trustees of the
British Museum
Published by
British Museum Press
A division of British Museum
Publications Ltd
46 Bloomsbury Street,
London WC1B 3QQ
British Library Cataloguing
in Publication Data
Cherry, John
    Goldsmiths. – (Medieval
    craftsmen)
    I. Title
    739.22092
ISBN 0-7141-2055-3
Designed by Roger Davies
Phototypeset by Southern
Positives and Negatives
(SPAN), Lingfield, Surrey
Printed and bound in
Singapore

In memory of Caspar, bringer
of gold.

Front cover: St Eligius at work
by Niclaus Manuel, 1515.
See Fig. 21.

Back cover: St Dunstan in his
workshop. See Fig. 59.

Title page: The Goldsmith and
the Young Couple, by Petrus
Christus, painted in 1449. The
importance of the goldsmith is
shown by the richness of his
varied stock: it includes
brooches, pearls, pieces of
crystal, red coral, cups, a belt
buckle and a small box of
rings.

This page: St Eligius as a
goldsmith, attributed to
Taddeo Gaddi. See Fig. 60.

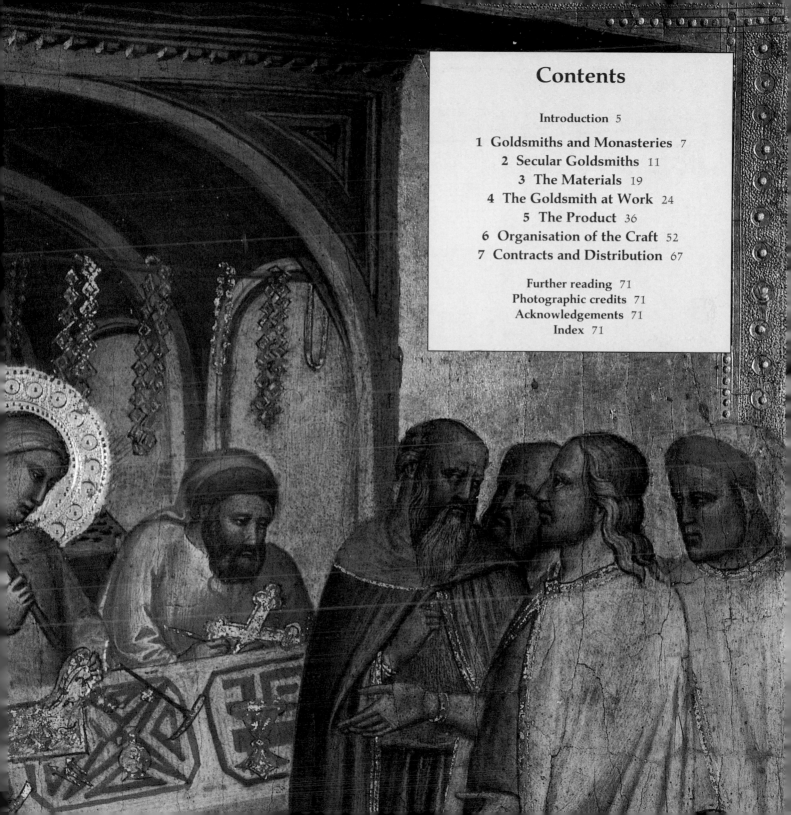

Contents

INTRODUCTION

Of all the medieval craftsmen the goldsmith worked upon the most precious metals, enriching them further with rare stones and engraved gems. Goldsmiths worked gold and silver into rings, brooches, vessels and precious ornaments in western Europe in the Middle Ages. Sometimes they worked in copper alloy which they decorated with enamelling and gilding. There was no separate term for silversmiths. The craftsmen were both monastic and secular, and ranged in wealth and success from poor apprentices to some of the richest craftsmen of the Middle Ages. Such wealth stemmed from the nature of the two precious metals with which they worked. In the words of Psalm 12 verse 6:

The words of the Lord are unalloyed:
silver refined in a crucible,
gold purified seven times over.

The comparison of the purity of the word of God with the fineness of the metals shows the high regard in which gold and silver were held in Biblical times and which continued through the Classical world to the Middle Ages and beyond; they were symbols of the divine. The appreciation of gold as a metal suitable for kings and nobles in the medieval period is shown, for example, by Wolfram von Eschenbach, the German poet who flourished around 1200, who, describing the feast at the Court of King Arthur attended by Parzifal (or Percival), tells how Gawain's cupbearer ordered pages to bring many costly goblets of gold adorned with precious stones.

Abbot Suger of Saint-Denis, north of Paris, (abbot from 1122 until his death in 1151), justified his patronage of gorgeous and elaborate vestments and goldsmiths' work by arguing that such display praised God through the outward ornaments of sacred vessels and that it was worth man's effort to cover reliquaries, which often contained the sacred ashes of saints, with the most precious materials possible. His account of his administration of the Abbey was written between 1144 and 1146/7

and more than eighty per cent of it is given to an account of the holy vessels, the altar furniture, the great golden crucifix and the restoration of the other possessions of the Abbey. A chalice which Suger added to the treasury of Saint-Denis has survived: it is an antique agate fluted bowl, to which a silver-gilt knop and foot have been added, held in place by two handles joining them to the rim. The chalice remained in the Treasury of Saint-Denis until the French Revolution and illustrates how medieval goldsmiths' work is still appreciated today in museums and church treasuries.

Who were the goldsmiths who produced these objects? Were they monastic or secular? How did they obtain their materials and from where? What techniques did they use? What objects did they make? How were goldsmiths in towns organised? How did they control their craft? How did they sell and distribute their products?

Four types of evidence can be used to answer these questions: written, pictorial, archaeological and the objects themselves. Among the written sources is the excellent working manual *De Diversis Artibus* by the twelfth-century monk Theophilus. It has been described as 'the first European writing in which there is realistic detail on a wide range of technical processes'. It was written between 1110 and 1140, possibly shortly after 1122–3. The first book is concerned with painting, the second with glass-making, and the third with metalworking. The detailed knowledge revealed in it could only have been acquired by an experienced metalworker. The preface to the third part of the book, written in stylish Latin, reflects on the role of beauty in the House of the Lord. Theophilus indicates that it is through the working of the Holy Spirit manifested in the seven attributes of wisdom, understanding, counsel, fortitude, knowledge, godliness and the fear of the Lord, that beautiful and rich art can be made which will proclaim the wonderfulness of God. In particular, the craftsman is to create

1 The richly decorated chalice of Abbot Suger. An antique agate fluted vase, probably second century BC, was mounted in the twelfth century with silver gilt adorned with filigree and precious stones.

those vessels essential to the services in the Church which praise God: chalices, candlesticks, censers, cruets, shrines, reliquaries, crosses, and covers for Gospel Books. While this preface may not seem to say anything particularly unusual, it must be seen in the context of the arguments between the Benedictine Cluniac monks and the Cistercians, particularly St Bernard of Clairvaux. St Bernard's *Apology*, written in 1122–3, attacked the lavish ornamentation of monastic churches and the treatise of Theophilus may have been part of the continuing argument by the Benedictines against that view.

Alexander of Neckham (1157–1217), an Englishman who taught in Paris, also wrote a description of a twelfth-century goldsmith's workshop. However, for the later medieval period there is not such descriptive evidence, although there are occasional contracts for the manufacture of specific objects which give the name of the goldsmith and the method of manufacture. The most common written source for the activities of goldsmiths are the accounts of payments for their products preserved in the archives of their patrons – kings, dukes, wealthy nobles and bishops. An additional source is the inventories sometimes included in wills of merchants and nobles. Gold and silver vessels are listed in the inventories of such people. These were often written down when they died or when the official responsible for the care of the precious objects changed. Such accounts and inventories are more common in the later medieval period, but, save in one or two very rare exceptions, the entries do not name the goldsmiths and cannot be associated with surviving objects. The last major written source is the records of the guilds who attempted to control the activities of those working in gold and silver. While this evidence is useful in indicating what goldsmiths should not do, or were not meant to do, it is perhaps less useful in showing what they actually did.

Pictorial evidence includes sculptures, paintings, woodcuts, engravings and occasionally manuscripts. Artists painted depictions of gold-smiths and their saints. These depictions some- [21, 22, 58, 60] times show St Dunstan or St Eligius, the two patron saints of goldsmiths, and occasionally show secular goldsmiths. The most common portrayal is that of the legend of St Eligius which sometimes appears in paintings commissioned by guilds of goldsmiths and which shows the [74] goldsmith in his shop or workshop.

Archaeological evidence for the goldsmith is likely to increase as work continues. It takes two forms. The first is the study of tools and instruments used in the manufacture of the objects. These are hammers, moulds and crucibles. The second is the evidence of sites. Unfortunately for this type of evidence, the workshops of the goldsmith were housed in buildings and, unlike the potter or the tiler, did not leave extensive traces of kilns.

The fourth type of evidence is that of the objects themselves. Very little surviving [57] medieval goldsmiths' work is dated and it is often very difficult to assign individual pieces to their place of origin. Unlike modern goldsmiths' work, which is often marked with the date, maker and place of origin, a system of marks to [64] indicate date and town of origin developed only gradually in the Middle Ages. Some exceptional medieval pieces have the name of the craftsman upon them, for example, the Sienese chalice, but [71] this is most unusual.

There is a considerable amount of information, derived from legal records or the records of craft organisations, which gives the goldsmiths' names, heirs, places of work and home, official positions, and importance in the craft. However, there is an almost total absence of information concerning the questions that the historian of objects would most want to ask – how the goldsmiths developed their skill, what influenced them, how much freedom did they have in design, and what were their artistic relations with other goldsmiths. This book will summarise our knowledge of medieval gold-smiths but the lack of information means that some of the most interesting questions must remain unanswered.

1 GOLDSMITHS AND MONASTERIES

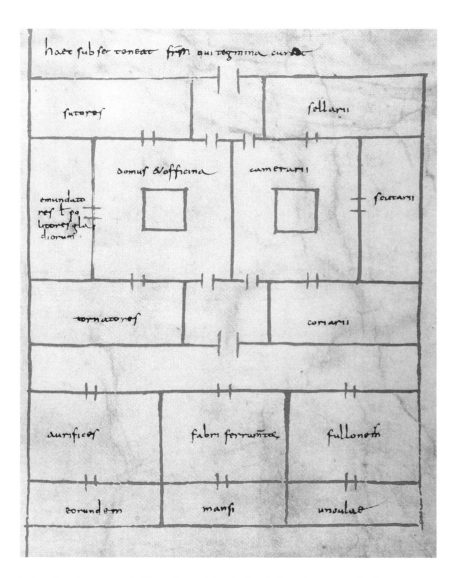

haec sub se teneat frm qui regmina curae

sutores   sellarii

domus &officina   camerarii

emundato
res t po
licoret pla
diorum   scutarii

tornatores   coriarii

aurifices   fabri ferramen   fullones

eorundem   mansi   unsulae

2 The plan of the annex to the main workshop in the ninth-century monastic plan preserved at the Abbey of St Gall, Switzerland. The annex contained the workshops of the goldsmiths, *aurifices*, blacksmiths, *fabri ferram'tor'*, and fullers, *fullones*.

Monasteries played an important part in the transmission of culture during the period of economic growth and recovery following the destruction caused by the Viking invasions of the eighth and ninth centuries. The Benedictine Abbey of St Gall in Switzerland possesses a ninth-century plan of an ideal monastery. This [2] shows not only the great church and cloister with the dormitory and refectory but also a series of ancillary buildings. A collection of workshops, one of which was assigned to the goldsmiths, lay on the south of the Abbey church beyond the cloister, between the granary on one side and the monks' bake and brew house and the mill on the other. The goldsmiths were placed in an annex to the main workshop, beside the blacksmiths, perhaps because both activities involved fire hazards. Their living quarters were reached through the workshops.

Monasteries were a major source of patronage for goldsmiths because of the demand for gold and silver objects used for the services in the church. In the period up to the early thirteenth century some goldsmiths were monks, for instance, Theophilus, the writer of the treatise *De Diversis Artibus*. Roger of Hel-[26] marshausen, who made a portable altar for Henry of Werl, Bishop of Paderborn, in 1100, worked for the monastery. In return for his work, the Abbey received a local church and other tithes. According to some scholars, Roger of Helmarshausen may have been the same person as Theophilus. Hugo d'Oignies, who presented a manuscript with elaborate silver book covers to the monastery of Oignies near [3] Namur around 1230, is shown on the cover as a lay brother presenting the work to Saint Nicolaus, the patron saint of the monastery. However, it would be wrong to imagine that every great monastery in Europe at this time had a school of goldsmiths, or even a succession of schools, working for them.

Much is known about the great Benedictine monastery of St Albans in Hertfordshire because of the writings of Matthew Paris. He was a [18]

3 Silver book covers of a set of gospels, made *c.*1228–30, inscribed as the work, both interior and exterior, of Brother Hugo d'Oignies. He is shown on the cover (bottom dark panel on the left edge) presenting a book to Saint Nicolaus, the patron saint of the priory of Oignies.

goldsmith, who became a monk in 1217 and died in 1259. On his death it was said that he possessed such skill in gold and silver and other metals, that it was believed that he left no equal in the Latin world after him. This may have been more a conventional form of praise rather than an accurate estimate of his actual performance, although it is impossible to judge since no work can be ascribed to him. However, the evidence for the work of goldsmiths at St Albans begins in the twelfth century. Abbot Geoffrey wished to start work on a shrine to St Alban and put the work in the hands of a monk called Anketyl, who was to be assisted by a young lay assistant, Salamon of Ely. Anketyl had spent seven years in Denmark working for the Danish king as a goldsmith and controlling the royal mint. That the task of making such an important shrine should have been given to a craftsman trained abroad and that his assistant should come from elsewhere suggests that the goldsmiths' craft was not popular among the monks of St Albans. Anketyl may have been responsible for the other works presented by Abbot Geoffrey to the Abbey which included three silver cruets and one of crystal, silver-gilt candlesticks, an arm reliquary, a chalice and paten weighing eight marks of gold (sufficiently impressive to be sent later as a gift to Pope Celestine in 1143–4) and a gold and silver altarpiece of fine workmanship and set with choice gems for the high altar.

Later in the twelfth century, another Abbot of St Albans, Simon, wanted to cover the shrine of St Alban with silver-gilt for which he employed two goldsmiths. The first, John of St Albans, was probably the King's Goldsmith, while the second, Master Baldwin, was a most eminent goldsmith (*aurifaber praeelectus*) but not a member of the community. Master Baldwin's masterpiece, according to the chronicles of St Albans, was a large chalice of pure gold 'of which there was none more noble in England' and which was 'set with precious stones suitable to a work in such a material, embellished with a most subtle design of intricate flowers'.

A craftsman who became a monk in the early thirteenth century was Walter of Colchester, a sculptor and painter as well as a goldsmith. For

4 Lead pilgrim badge of the shrine of Saint Thomas à Becket, richly decorated with gems. A small figure (under the ship on the right) points to the large ruby given by the King of France.

the Abbey of St Albans he made a frontal for the high altar and two silver-gilt book covers on one of which was the Crucifixion between the Virgin and St John and on the other Christ in Majesty between the emblems of the four evangelists (which may have resembled the book cover of Hugo d'Oignies).

One of his major works was the provision of three images for the shrine of St Thomas à Becket at Canterbury for which the King allowed him from 250 to 350 marks from the revenues of the archbishopric of Canterbury in November 1243. The shrine and its contents were thoroughly obliterated by Henry VIII but the report of the Venetian ambassador in 1500 gives an idea of the impressive appearance of one of the greatest pieces of English goldsmiths' work:

Notwithstanding its great size, it is entirely covered over with plates of pure gold, but the gold is scarcely visible from the variety of precious stones with which it is studded, such as sapphires, diamonds, rubies, balas-rubies, and emeralds, and on every side that the eye turns,

something more beautiful than the other appears. And these beauties of nature are enhanced by human skill, for the gold is carved and engraved in beautiful designs, both large and small, and agates, jaspers and cornelians set in relievo, some of the cameos being of such size that I do not dare to mention it, but everything is left behind by a ruby, not larger than a thumb nail, which is set to the right of the altar. The church is rather dark, and particularly so where the shrine is placed, and when we went to see it the sun was nearly gone down, and the weather was cloudy, yet I saw that ruby as if·I had it in my hand. They say it was the gift of a King of France.

The shrine in the late fourteenth century is represented on a lead pilgrim's sign and the mould carver has shown it covered in precious stones. 4

It is clear that while such a rich abbey as St Albans would require much goldsmiths' work for liturgical purposes or for gifts, there is little evidence for a monastic school of goldsmiths since we know of only five monastic goldsmiths at St Albans and, though there may have been more, there was certainly no continuity of supply of such work. An abbot would have been pleased at the admission of a trained goldsmith to the brotherhood since this would save the expense of employing an outsider.

In the fourteenth and fifteenth centuries there appears to have been a decline in the artistic output of monasteries including goldsmiths' work. This is less likely to have been due to a failure of the goldsmith monks to impart their skills to their successors than to the fact that goldsmiths had ceased to train as monks. We shall see later for example that the Abbot of Bury St Edmunds ordered a splendid new crozier from a London goldsmith in 1430. The goldsmiths of the later Middle Ages were men of the world not of the cloister.

5 This elaborate golden reliquary, the Holy Thorn Reliquary, is decorated with white enamelled figures *en ronde bosse*. It was commissioned from a Parisian goldsmith *c*.1405 by Jean, Duke of Berry (*d*.1416), whose arms are on the castellated base. The thorn from the Crown of Thorns is placed at the very centre behind a 'window' of rock crystal.

2 SECULAR GOLDSMITHS

It is most likely that secular goldsmiths worked for emperors, kings and nobles in royal and aristocratic courts and that there were separate urban goldsmiths. William of Poitiers, a Norman chronicler, described the court held by William the Conqueror at Fécamp at Easter 1067 and tells how the noblemen of northern France were struck with wonderment at William's splendid robes and at the 'gold and silver vessels, of whose number and beauty things incredible could be truthfully related'. It is as a result of the growth of towns through increased trade in the eleventh and twelfth centuries that the number of urban goldsmiths grew. The twelfth century witnessed more and more goldsmiths in London, Paris and other major European cities. In 1180 eighteen London guilds were heavily fined by the Crown for being associations formed without the permission of the Crown; of this sum (£120), one quarter was paid by the goldsmiths who were the richest of the eighteen guilds.

The goldsmiths of Paris were described by Jean de Garlande in his *Dictionary* written in the 1220s (trans. R. W. Lightbown):

The goldsmiths sit before their furnaces and tables on the Grand-Pont and make hanaps of gold and silver and brooches and pins and buttons, and chose garnets and jasper, sapphires and emeralds for rings. The skill of the goldsmiths hammers out gold and silver sheets with slender hammers on iron anvils. It sets precious gems in the bezels of rings that barons and noblemen wear. The craftsmen who are called hanapiers sheath vessels [of wood] in sheets of gold and silver and put feet under bowls, which they crown with circles [rims of precious metal] so that they may be lovelier, stronger, more durable and more saleable.

The siting of goldsmiths' shops on bridges, which also occurred at Florence on the Ponte Vecchio, shows how important it was for them to have their shops in places suitable for catching the passing trade of the town. The London goldsmiths were centred around 73 Cheapside, the principal street leading east from St Paul's Cathedral. There was further increase in trade and urban expansion in the late thirteenth and early fourteenth centuries which created a need for the regulation of the members and activities of the guilds of craftsmen. In Paris this led to the regulations drawn up by Etienne Boileau, the Prévost (mayor) of Paris in c.1268, and known as the *Livre des Métiers* (Book of Crafts). This document was of great importance for the development of similar regulations in other European towns. In 1292, when a tax list was drawn up for the whole of Paris, known as the *Livre de la Taille*, 116 goldsmiths and jewellers were listed. There was a similar expansion of the goldsmiths' craft in other French towns, which is revealed by the need to have distinguishing marks to ascertain the place of origin of a piece of silver. In 1275 the French King Philippe le Hardi (reigned 1270–85) ordered that in all towns where silversmiths worked in silver, they should work in refined silver, and that each town should have a mark to mark the silver. By the first half of the fourteenth century, marks are known from a number of French towns including Grenoble, Toulouse, Tours, Rouen, Carcassonne, Arras and Albi. In Britain the London mark is recorded in 1300, and the expansion in the number of goldsmiths in the first half of the fourteenth century is indicated by the acquisition of a Royal Charter by the London Company of Goldsmiths in 1327. By 1368 there were some 135 goldsmiths in the Company.

The number of goldsmiths increased throughout Europe until the Black Death in 1348, declined after that terrible event but then gradually increased in the course of the fifteenth century. Goldsmiths' work flourished in the great towns of Europe, such as Bruges, Utrecht, Lübeck, Florence and Strasbourg. In Germany 13 the largest concentration of goldsmiths was to be found in Cologne where in 1395 there were 122 masters, a number that remained constant until the early sixteenth century. Leo of Rozmital, a visitor to London in 1465, commented on the great number of goldsmiths in the city:

'The masters alone, without the journeymen, amount to four hundred, but they are never idle for the size of the city and its wealth provide them with work in abundance'.

Royal patronage was of great importance for the London goldsmiths, for example, since kings not only attempted to control the supply and quality of precious metals and the coinage but also provided orders for gold and silver plate, for the royal seals, and for shrines and crosses that were to be given to churches and monasteries. Henry III of England, who reigned from 1227 to 1272, was a generous donor to the architectural projects of English churches and religious orders, and he gave the works of many goldsmiths for the use and adornment of religious institutions. After 1240 the primary focus of his patronage was upon works for Westminster Abbey where he combined his interest in the arts with his deep veneration of the Westminster saint and his own personal patron saint, Edward the Confessor. He also intended to create at Westminster a burial place for the English kings at the shrine of King Edward that would emulate the burial place of the French kings at Saint-Denis. Henry's principal protégé was the goldsmith William of Gloucester who served as a supplier, artist and royal clerk. He appears for the first time in the royal records in 1251 when he received money for the labour and the precious metals that he used in a chalice for the King and for the repair of crystal candlesticks.

Later in the same year he supplied more than £55 worth of jewels and eleven garlands of gold worth £58 for the royal wedding festivities at York. In December 1252 he was designated as the King's Goldsmith, and the payments made after this include 110 marks for a crown given by Henry to the King of Norway and smaller sums for jewels, and for work on six cups for the King's half sister, Alice of Lusignan. There followed many commissions and sales which illustrate the wide series of requirements of a medieval king: brooches, rings (141 in 1253 alone), girdles, almsdishes, censers, chalices, mitres, croziers, thuribles, dishes, saucers and goblets. In addition to making a large number of individual objects, such as censers and chalices

for St Edward, an almsdish for Eleanor of Castile, a mitre and crozier for the Bishop of London and plate for the royal table, William was involved in projects of wider scope. The first of these was the production of the gold pennies of Henry III, the first English gold coinage, in 1257. His name is stamped as the moneyer on the reverse of the coins. The obverse of these coins shows a fine and detailed representation of Henry seated on his throne and holding his sceptre and orb. A similar seated figure occurs on the Great Seal that William was ordered to engrave in 1259. This seal was used from 1259 until 1272 and differs from earlier seals in that the King sits on an ornate Gothic throne and a sceptre is substituted for the usual sword.

The gold pennies and the impressions of the seal of 1259 are the only surviving examples of William's work. He was involved in other important royal commissions, notably for the altar frontal for the altar of St Edward for which he supplied many jewels with their settings, and the manufacture of a silver image of Katherine, the young daughter of Henry III, who was buried at Westminster in 1257. At Westminster he was also involved in the manufacture of the golden shrine of St Edward which was placed above the elaborately decorated base. For the last three years of his life he was occupied almost exclusively with this new shrine. He died in 1269 before it was finished, but the completed

6 Obverse (left) and reverse of a gold penny of Henry III struck c.1257. The moneyer was William of Gloucester, the King's Goldsmith.

7 Impression of the second Great Seal of Henry III, designed and made in silver in 1259 by William of Gloucester.

shrine into which the body of the saint was translated in October 1269 must have owed much to the design and skill of William of Gloucester.

William profited greatly from the position he held. He received important positions in the London and Canterbury mints, as well as exemptions from taxation and numerous commissions and sales. His role as citizen of London was, however, not always compatible with loyalty to the King since he opposed the King in the baronial wars that ended in the royal victory at the battle of Evesham in 1265, and he was imprisoned at Windsor. He had clearly made his peace with the King for in 1267 he was back in full favour and working at Westminster. He obtained property in London and owned manors in Kent and Essex. His success illustrates the way in which a goldsmith's career could be developed by the patronage of the king.

Another goldsmith who illustrates different aspects of the secular medieval goldsmith is Sir Edmund Shaa (the name is an early version of Shaw), who died in 1488 after a long and successful career. He was not the son of a long-established London goldsmith's family but a Cheshire boy who came to London to be apprenticed to a London goldsmith, William Botiller. In 1462 Shaa was appointed engraver to the Tower and other royal mints, including the one at Calais. He held these offices for twenty years until he relinquished them in favour of his nephew John Shaa. He was Warden of the Goldsmiths' Company in 1467 and 1471 and Prime Warden in 1476. The year 1483 was the climax of Sir Edmund Shaa's career for he served as Mayor of London and was also knighted for his support for Richard III.

His will indicates both that he did very well out of his craft, and that he was a very charitable man. He had a great house in Wood Street, London, as well as two Essex manor houses, Ardern Hall and Horndon House. He provided for his family by leaving £2000 to his wife together with all his household goods save his plate and jewels and all the tools belonging to his shop and warehouses. His charity is shown by the bequest of 400 marks for the making of a new stone gate at Cripplegate in the part of the

city wall built by the goldsmiths. The gate was to bear both his and the Company's arms. This work was carried out in 1490/1 and the form of it can be seen in an eighteenth-century engraving. There was a bequest of £20 in marriage portions to poor maidens and another £20 for the upkeep of the roads to Horndon, and a large number of individual bequests. He left money to be invested in property to provide income for a chantry where the priest would say a daily mass for the souls of Shaa's own family, for Edward IV, for Edward's sister, the late Duchess of Exeter, and in the words of the will 'for all the souls I am bound to pray for'. Further property was purchased and the income assigned for various purposes including refreshments for goldsmiths attending his obituary service and the sum of £10 for a man to teach grammar in a school at Stockport in Cheshire. This teacher was to have no other employment and it seems to be the first provincial grammar school started by a Londoner and supervised by a London Company.

Shaa's will also made provision for sixteen rings to be made of fine gold, each engraved with the five wells of sacred gifts – namely pity, mercy, comfort, grace and everlasting life – representing the five wounds of Christ. These were to be given to sixteen specified mourners. We know exactly what these rings look like, since such a ring was found at Coventry in the early nineteenth century. It illustrates the type of ring which Shaa records in his will that his two ex-apprentices, John Shaa and Raff Lathum, 'understand right well the making'.

John Shaa was Edmund's nephew and eventually inherited his manors and estates. John surpassed the achievements of his uncle becoming Joint Master of the Mint and a Member of Parliament, as well as a knight and Mayor of London. The careers of the Shaa goldsmiths show how their wealth and financial ability led to their taking important positions not only in their guild but also in local and national government.

A few of the more prominent goldsmiths were able, like Sir Edmund Shaa, to play a political role. Their property, and the close connection of the goldsmith with the coinage and

8 *Left* A nineteenth-century painting showing Sir Edmund Shaa offering the crown to Richard III in 1483. Painted by Sigismund Goetze for the Royal Exchange, London.

9 *Right* The north front of the new stone gate at Cripplegate, built in 1490–1, at the expense of Sir Edmund Shaa.

hence the medieval management of economic matters, made them suitable candidates. However, the goldsmiths' craft was not necessarily a prosperous one and included a wide range of people. Research in Utrecht suggests that only ten per cent of the 280 people named as goldsmiths in the surviving medieval documents would have qualified to become involved in city politics. In most cases this was as an alderman of the guild or a member of the city council. There are no depictions of these particular goldsmiths, but portraits do survive of one or two from the fifteenth century. An impressive one is the early work by Jan van Eyck

which he painted in 1436 of John de Leeuw, Dean of the goldsmiths' guild at Bruges. He is shown holding a ring set with a stone, which may be either an indication of his engagement or his craft. A later, rather more sympathetic, portrait of a goldsmith is by the Bruges painter Gerard David of *c*.1500. Here the goldsmith looks at someone to the left of the viewer of the painting. Perhaps he is looking at the person to whom he is offering the ring that he has just drawn off the roll of parchment that he holds in his left hand. The fine dress of both men is an indication of the prosperity of the successful Flemish goldsmiths of the late Middle Ages.

10 *Above* An early sixteenth-century gold ring found at Coventry showing the Five Wounds of Christ and the Resurrection. This is very similar to the sixteen rings that Sir Edmund Shaa ordered to be made for his mourners.

11 Portrait of an unknown goldsmith painted around 1500 by Gerard David of Bruges.

13 *Right* Silver beaker made by the goldsmith Hans Timmerman of Lübeck in the early sixteenth century. The subjects on the upper zone are copied, with slight variations, from engravings by the Master ES. They include Samson rending the lion, the woman of Timnath, a pair of lovers embracing, a fool playing bagpipes, a lady reading a letter to a fool, and a wild woman and a unicorn.

12 *Opposite* Silver lid of a cup decorated with *champlevé* and translucent enamels. It was probably made *c.*1300 by a Parisian goldsmith and enameller as a gift from King Philip IV of France to Raoul de Nesle, Constable of France, who married Isabelle of Hainault in 1297.

14 *Left* The miners of Kuttenberg as shown on the frontispiece of the Kuttenberger Kanzional by Matthaus of Kuttenberg, *c.*1490. This was at one time the richest in Europe. The illustration shows all the processes of metal extraction from underground mining to ore crushing, grading the ore and finally the selling of the ore.

15 *Below* Detail of the Kuttenberger Kanzional showing a group of men wearing little clothing. They are washing themselves after work and reporting to the foreman, who is dressed in a red cloak and is recording their day's work by cutting notches on a tally stick.

3 THE MATERIALS

Gold and silver, the two precious metals, were the principal materials of the goldsmith. Gold occurs as a native metal either as veins in quartz rocks or in sediments derived from the weathering of those rocks. The simplest, although very tedious, way of recovering gold from the sands and beds of rivers was by 'panning'. In this process, sand was placed on a shallow dish with water and the dish swirled around so that the lighter quartz floated to the edge and the heavier gold stayed in the middle. Theophilus describes this way of gathering gold from the sand found on the banks of the River Rhine. After panning, the gold was put in a vessel to which quicksilver (mercury) was added and mixed. The mixture was put in a fine cloth, the quicksilver squeezed out, and the remains placed in a crucible and fired. Panning was also used to recover mined gold, especially where the veins were thin – the gold-bearing quartz would be crushed to a small particle size and then washed to recover the gold.

In the early medieval period, western and central Europe produced very little gold. In the ancient world stocks of gold had steadily accumulated for, short of burying it in hoards or in graves, or throwing it away, its imperishable nature meant that it was constantly recycled. The gold used by a goldsmith in London or Paris in the fourteenth century may well have included gold which had previously been used in an Arab coin, a Byzantine cross, Roman or even Egyptian jewellery. The collapse of the Roman Empire did not bring to an end the use of gold in the West, for the barbarian kingdoms that replaced the Empire continued to mint and use gold coins and fashion gold jewellery until around AD 700. The use of gold in this period most probably depended on existing stocks rather than any new supply. The decline in the use of gold in the West after about AD 700 was due to the economic strength of Byzantium in the East which served to attract gold to it. The supply of luxury goods from Constantinople such as textiles – cotton, linen and silk – was paid for in gold, and it is notable that the Byzantine emperors accumulated great wealth in gold. Emperor Anastasius, for example, left at his death in AD 518 a personal treasure of 320,000 lbs of gold. Consequently, in the five hundred years after AD 700 western Europe lacked gold and thus silver became the main precious metal from which coins were minted.

The rich gold-bearing areas of Nigeria and the Gold Coast in West Africa were opened up by the expansion of the Arab empire westwards along the north African coast, trading and using the gold coinage that they had established under the Ummayad dynasty at Damascus in the seventh century. From the eighth century Timbuktu in the western Sahara became active as a collecting centre for the gold that was washed from the topmost reaches of the Niger and Senegal rivers. This gold was then taken by camel either to the ports of north Africa or across the Sahara to Egypt. The emergence of this gold enabled the Arabs to mint gold coins from the seventh century onwards and later to expand the coinage. Theophilus refers to such Arabian gold as being of an exceptional red colour.

The Crusaders, from the twelfth century onwards, were responsible for taking large quantities of silver coinage to the Latin kingdoms of the eastern Mediterranean. These kingdoms, however, began to mint gold coins and thus attract gold away from the neighbouring Arab countries. In the thirteenth century Italian cities such as Genoa, Florence, and Naples exported silver and received gold in return in the form of Arab coins. This may have been the principal factor behind the introduction of new gold currencies in Europe in this period. Gold coins were minted in Florence in 1252, in France in 1254, Sicily and Naples in 1278, and Venice in 1284. Even England under Henry III (r.1227–72), not to be outdone by France, attempted the introduction of a gold coinage, organised by William of Gloucester (see above). Some of the gold used in these western

16 Silver-gilt brooch of the late fourteenth century in the form of a crowned letter M with figures of the Archangel Gabriel and the Virgin Mary framed in the double arch of the letter.

European gold coins may have come from newly discovered or exploited sources in Europe itself. In the thirteenth century gold was being washed from the Rhine valley, Silesia, and Bohemia, but the quantities involved were very small. At that time, the main part of the supplies of gold was controlled or distributed by the Arab powers in the Mediterranean. This process of distribution was carried out through commerce, and the new gold currencies of western Europe could only succeed if production and trade were increased. The gold coins of Florence and Venice succeeded at a time when the experimental gold coinage of Henry III in England failed.

In the fourteenth and fifteenth centuries, there was a need for more gold. This was satisfied not only by imports from the Arab world but also by an increased European production from mining.

European production was not, however, very considerable at first. The sinking of mine shafts in the auriferous belt from the Rhine to the Carpathians became possible because of the development of water-wheels to take away excess water and prevent flooding. The first mine to produce gold in Europe was that at Trenmitz in Bohemia, which was discovered in the 1320s. It has been estimated that Silesia, Bohemia, Thuringia and the eastern Alps may not have produced, in the whole of the fifteenth century, more than 50,000 lbs of gold among them. Although gold had been mined in Wales in the Roman period there is no evidence of gold mining in Britain between the Roman period and the sixteenth century. Hungary was the major producer in the later Middle Ages and a gold currency was minted there from 1324/5. Hungary's output rose steadily from the thirteenth to the sixteenth centuries and has been estimated at between 2000 and 5000 lbs annually. A Hungarian scholar suggested that in the later Middle Ages eleven twelfths of Europe's gold production came from Bohemia and Hungary and by far the greater part of this from Hungary.

No actual ingots or gold bars are known from the medieval period, though they certainly existed for in 1294 when the monks of the

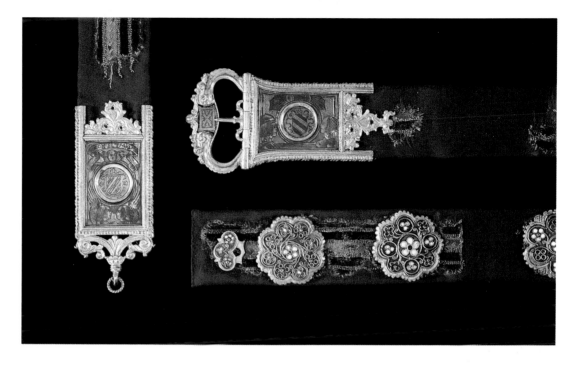

Bavarian monastery of Aldersbach wished to make a contribution to their abbot in Paris, they bought gold ingots in exchange for silver and sent them to him. Therefore, it is likely that the main way in which the goldsmith received his gold would not have been in the form of ingots but as gold coins, either bezants (Byzantine gold coins) or dinars, the coins used in Moslem Spain or north Africa.

Silver is the second precious metal. In contrast to gold, silver was produced continuously in western Europe. The mines at Melle in Poitou in France provided metal for the Merovingian coinage. The silver mines of Sardinia attracted the attention of the Italian republics of Genoa and Pisa in the eleventh and twelfth centuries. The Rammelsberg silver mines above Goslar in Germany were a source of silver from the tenth to the twelfth centuries. In 1170 the discovery of the rich silver bearing ores of Freiberg in Saxony led to increased production. Production here continued until the fourteenth century. Albertus Magnus, the Dominican friar, referred to the purity of the silver found here in his *De Re Metallica* (Book of Minerals):

In this place it is found in earth as a sort of vein purer than any found in stone. It is sometimes found as soft as a firm mush, and this is the purest and best kind of silver, having very little slag, as if it had been purified by the industry of nature.

The richest European silver mines were discovered in the second half of the thirteenth century at Kuttenberg (Kutná Hora), some fifty miles east of Prague, and the considerable production of these mines probably financed the rich flowering of Czech culture at the end of the Middle Ages. It has been estimated that about one quarter of the production of the silver here was minted and that the rest was exported in bars. The mining, refining and assaying activities at Kuttenberg are dramatically illustrated in the frontispiece of the Kuttenberger 14, 15 Kanzional by Matthaus of Kuttenberg c.1490. However, the Hussite wars of the early fifteenth century left the Bohemian mining town in ruins. It appears that in the fifteenth century the production of silver here declined.

Just as gold could be melted down and reused

so also could silver. In England, silver was obtained as a by-product of lead mining since galena (lead sulphide) contained small quantities of silver. In the thirteenth century there was a small silver mine at Buckland in north Devon which operated in the 1260s and produced about one third of a ton of silver per year. The Devon silver and lead mines were very productive over the half century from 1290 to 1340. From 1292 to 1297, the Devon mines produced £4046 of silver and about £360 worth of lead. After mining, the mixture of silver and lead had to be refined. The silver was then cast into plates or ingots varying from ten to twenty pounds in weight and value. The purity of refined silver probably varied. For instance 370 lbs of silver sent up from Martinstowe in 1294 had to be further refined in London before it could be made into silver vessels for the Countess of Barre.

What were the sources of the stones set into the gold and silver? Both cameos and intaglios were highly prized in the Classical world, and many survived into the Middle Ages to be set into rings, seals and other pieces of metalwork. Cameos were precious stones with differently coloured layers, where the upper layer was cut away to form the design leaving the lower as a background; intaglios were stones into which a design was deeply engraved. Classical gems may have been found at Roman towns such as St Albans. At St Albans, there was preserved a great cameo that was given to the Abbey by King Aethelred. It has not survived but a 18 realistic drawing by Matthew Paris still exists. It probably shows the Roman Emperor Augustus and was made after his death in the first half of the first century AD. Other cameos and gems were recovered from older goldsmiths' work and reused. One of the most striking illustrations of the use of classical cameos is on the crown worn in 1257 by Richard, Earl of Cornwall, when he was crowned King of the Romans in the Cathedral at Aachen where it is still preserved. Medieval gem-cutters produced both cameos and intaglios for use in seals and rings.

The principal source of the main precious stones such as rubies and sapphires in the

18 Matthew Paris' drawing of the great cameo of St Albans Abbey, the sardonyx gem given to the Abbey by King Aethelred. Paris, who described it in the 1250s, records that the cameo was efficacious in childbirth since as it was drawn down the mother's body, the unborn babe fled from its approach out into the world.

medieval period was from the East. Rubies came 31, 32 from India and Ceylon; sapphires from Ceylon, Arabia and Persia. Emeralds came from Egypt and turquoises from Persia or Tibet, and amethysts from Germany or Russia. Diamonds were rare in the early Middle Ages but became more common in the fourteenth and fifteenth centuries. They came either from India or Central Africa. Traders in stones from the East came through the Mediterranean and it is clear that the Jewish community in Italy played a considerable part. There exists a list of precious stones with their prices compiled by a Jewish merchant in 1453. The interest of the list is not only that it shows that Jews were dealing in precious stones but also that there was a wide trade in less valuable and less grand stones. A glimpse of a richer part of this trade is obtained from the inventories of Jean, Duke of Berry, 53, 54 brother of King Charles v of France. He obtained rubies, emeralds, pearls and diamonds from 5 Nicolas Pigace, a Genoese merchant, and Loys

Gradenigo of Venice sold Jean Duke of Berry two famous diamonds in 1412 and presented him with a third as a gift.

One of the regulations of the Goldsmiths' Company states that if any merchant, either foreign or English, bears jewels for sale, the four Wardens of the craft are to inspect them to ensure that they are good and true so that the great men and the commonalty of the land are not deceived. Sometimes, goldsmiths themselves dealt in jewels. The inventory of Walter Pynchon (see p.69) includes unmounted stones and such stones can be seen in the painting of ^{title page} St Eligius and two visitors by Petrus Christus. (The exact meaning of the term jeweller in the late Middle Ages is unclear, and it may well have been applied to a variety of activities. It might mean a retailer of gemstones or a retailer of goldsmiths' work; it might, however, mean an appraiser of gemstones or simply the craftsmen who cut or set the stones.) In England William Russe (d.1434) is often referred to as a citizen and jeweller, and John Paddesley (d.1451) was owed £3150 by the King for jewels that had been bought to give to ambassadors in the previous three years.

Of the semi-precious stones and gems, some came from Europe. The sources of rock crystal are many but those mainly used in the Middle Ages were in Germany, Switzerland, and France. Opals and garnets came from eastern Europe. Pearls were found in freshwater mussels in rivers in Scotland; they were normally pierced for use and either mounted on metal or sewn onto clothing. Amber, the fossilised resin of pine trees, was washed up on the shores of the Baltic and was found in great quantities around Königsberg in northern Germany. Jet, the fossilised remains of trees, was found near coal measures both at Whitby in northern England and also in Spain. Coral came from the Mediterranean, particularly the north African coast, where the French had a fishery for it in 1450. Jet, amber and coral were all worked in London, particularly for the manufacture of rosaries. Fragments of all these, in different stages of working, have been found in the area of Paternoster Row, where the sellers of rosaries had their shops.

'Cabochon' gems were used on goldsmiths' and silversmiths' work. The cabochon effect was acquired by rubbing and polishing the stone. The technique of cutting in planes gives stones a more reflective and brilliant effect. By the fourteenth century diamonds were being turned into pointed stones by the simple method of halving the natural octahedron shape, and by the early fifteenth century simple patterns of diamond cutting were being employed. These included the hog-back, which was an oblong with sloping edges; the rosette, which was a combination of hog-backs; and the lozenge, a pattern of diamond-shaped cuts. Sapphires were also being engraved in the fourteenth century, particularly in Paris. Although the *Livre des Métiers* by Etienne Boileau, issued between 1258 and 1269 for the Paris Guild, still lists goldsmiths and jewellers together, the trade of the jeweller or the one who prepared the stone gradually grew into a more independent craft.

19 Two gold signet rings. The left one dates to the late fourteenth century; it is set with a ruby on each shoulder and is engraved on the bezel with a shield including the arms of the de Grailly family. The right one is French and dates to the fifteenth century; it is engraved with a Saracen's head and the legend *nul si bien*, 'none so well'.

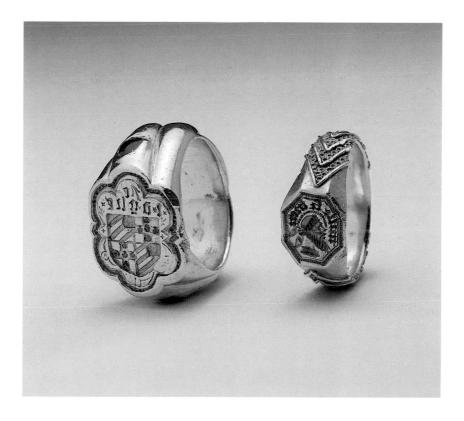

4 THE GOLDSMITH AT WORK

One of the most vivid descriptions of a medieval goldsmith's workshop was given by Alexander Neckham (see p.6). His lively description may reflect his personal observation of goldsmiths at work in Paris in the late twelfth century. In his words:

The goldsmith should have a furnace with a hole at the top so that the smoke can get out. One hand should govern the bellows with light pressure and with the greatest care so that the air pressed through the nozzle may blow upon the coals and feed the fire. Let him have an anvil of extreme hardness on which the iron or gold may be laid and softened and may take the required form. They can be stretched and pulled with the tongs and the hammer. There should also be a hammer for making gold leaf, as well as sheets of silver, tin, brass, iron or copper. The goldsmith must have a very sharp chisel with which he can engrave figures of many kinds on amber, hard stone, marble, emerald, sapphire or pearl. He should have a touchstone for testing, and one for distinguishing steel from iron. He must also have a rabbit's foot for smoothing, polishing and wiping the surface of gold and silver. The small particles of metal should be collected in a leather apron. He must have small pottery vessels and cruets, and a toothed saw and file for gold as well as gold and silver wire with which broken objects can be mended or properly constructed. He must also be as skilled in engraving as well as in bas relief, in casting and as well as in hammering. His apprentice must have a waxed table, or one covered with clay, for portraying little flowers and drawing in various ways. He must know how to distinguish pure gold from latten and copper, lest he buy latten for pure gold. For it is difficult to escape the wiliness of the fraudulent merchant.

Many of these tools can be seen in the representations of medieval goldsmiths at work. Perhaps the earliest is that of St Dunstan at work with hammer and anvil in an early fourteenth-century illustration. A similar simple portrayal 20 occurs in the Mendelschen Hausbuch written in Nuremberg in 1469. Here the goldsmith hammers the rim of a bowl against an anvil mounted in wood, beside a table on which stand the other main products of the goldsmith — a cup and cover and a ring. It is, however, the painting front cover, by Niclaus Manuel (1484–1530), dated 1515, 21 on the exterior of an altarpiece of the Virgin Mary that provides one of the most informative illustrations of the medieval goldsmith at work. This painting was ordered by the guild of painters and goldsmiths of Bern, Switzerland, for the Predigerkirche and shows the story of St Eligius. One goldsmith is shown working a ring with a chisel while the two visitors, St Eligius and his friend, are hammering a silver chalice on an anvil and working the bottom of a cup. On the low and broad bench between the goldsmiths lies a number of tools, notably chisels and dividers, and a shallow dish. There is a large box of weights and a curious vessel rather like an oil can, whose function is obscure. At the back the apprentice works the bellows for the furnace. The work takes place at a low bench near an open window. Despite the fact that this painting is some three hundred years after the

21 *Right* Saint Eligius at his work by Niclaus Manuel, 1515.

20 *Opposite* The goldsmith at work using a hammer and anvil to shape the rim of a bowl. On the table is a standing cup with cover on a tripod base, and a ring. From the Mendelschen Hausbuch, 1469.

25

22 A late-fifteenth-century goldsmith's workshop by the Master of Balaam showing St Eligius at work in the midst of confusion.

description by Neckham it is unlikely that there was any great change in the tools used or the manner of working.

The painting by Manuel shows St Eligius as a visitor to another goldsmith's workshop, but the engraving by the Master of Balaam shows St Eligius in his own workshop. Here he calmly concentrates on hammering the rim of a chalice while seated on a chair of suitable episcopal dignity. Everything around him is marked by disorder caused by the intrusion of folly. Birds copulate, dogs howl, a stool and shoe are upside down, a monkey sits on the window and a young girl wields a hammer with mighty force. Whatever the exact meaning of the iconography of this engraving, it provides a very different and possibly more realistic impression of the medieval goldsmith's workshop than the painting by Manuel. Finally, two representations of goldsmiths' workshops from the sixteenth century, engraved by Etienne Delaune (c.1518/19—83) in 1576, show the same general arrangement of tables, anvils, tools and furnaces. One of the main changes shown in these

engravings is the use of a four-handled lever to enable wire to be pulled through a drawplate, but it is likely that this was in fact introduced much earlier. The different sized holes in the drawplate enabled different gauges of wire to be drawn through it. Another new development shown in this engraving is that one of the goldsmiths is shown wearing glasses. Glasses were certainly worn in the fifteenth century, and the relationship of the development of lenses to goldsmiths' work remains an unexplored subject.

Theophilus' account of a goldsmith's workshop is most valuable. He is clearly writing for an ideal monastery. His description of the physical arrangements for the metalworkers may indicate an ideal, rarely achieved in real life. He writes that the workshop is to be spacious and lofty, with many windows, and divided into three sections, one for gold, one for silver and one for the casting process and for base metal. In front of each window there is to be a work table set in a sunken area lined with wood so that any particles of gold and silver can be

23 and **24** Engravings of silversmiths' workshops, by Etienne Delaune, Augsburg, 1576. They show the tools, activities and kiln of the silversmiths.

25 A goldsmith working at his furnace, with his bellows to hand, *c.*1220–30. He is hammering a piece of metalwork over an anvil.

26 *Below* A passage of Theophilus' *De Diversis Artibus* describing the seating accomodation for the workmen and the construction of the work furnace.

carefully removed. Each bench has its own work furnace beside it, with bellows made of rams' skins. He then refers to the tools and is far more explicit than Alexander of Neckham. For instance, he describes several different types of anvil. Some are broad, flat and square, or flat and horned; some are rounded above like half an apple; others are long and narrow like two barbs projecting from a spear of which one is round and tapered out so that it is narrow at the top, the other broader and slightly turned back at the top in a smooth curve like a thumb. There is not space here to go into the detail of his descriptions of the different types of hammers, pincers, files, chisels, rasps, chasing tools and scorpers, but a most interesting picture is drawn of the tools used by the medieval goldsmith. Draw-plates for making wires are briefly mentioned, but Theophilus describes at some length an implement called the *organarium* which consisted of two iron parts secured by pins. Each of the two inner faces of the two parts is carved with grooves and has cavities in the centre. When a piece of gold or silver wire is inserted between the two iron parts the upper is struck with a hammer and a bead of gold or silver produced. One of the longest series of chapters in *De Diversis Artibus* gives instructions on the manufacture, construction and embellishment of a chalice with niello and gilding.

Archaeology provides some evidence of workshop sites. Precious metals often had to be purified before use or reuse and archaeological evidence of this process has now been identified. Separating precious from base metals was achieved by 'cupellation' while silver was separated from gold by a process known as 'parting'. In the first, the metal was melted with a greater amount of lead which was oxidised, so forming litharge (lead oxide) which dissolved any base metals present, leaving just the gold and silver. The archaeological find which provides evidence for this is known as a 'litharge cake' (a dense grey or green circular lump of litharge). A number of these have been found on urban sites of Late Saxon and medieval date. Cupellation was carried out either on a bone ash bed or on a ceramic base. So far these ceramic bases have only been identified at Winchester, where an important series of excavations from 1961–71 produced a fine collection of the archaeological objects associated with the working of precious metals. Until the twelfth century, Winchester was the site of the royal treasury and this may have led to a particular concentration of precious metalworking. Touchstones and crucibles were found there and date to the ninth and tenth centuries and parts of heating trays and pieces of litharge of a later date were also found. No medieval bone ash cupels are known. The earliest that have been found are of sixteenth century date from the Tower of London.

A specialised vessel for 'parting', the separation of silver from gold, has only recently been recognised from tenth-century York. This vessel, cuboid in shape, would have contained sheets of mixed metal interleaved with crushed brick mixed up with salt. On heating, the salt reacted with the silver to form silver chloride which was deposited on the crushed brick. When the vessel cooled the gold could be removed and remelted, and the crushed brick smelted to recover the silver.

Sites which have yielded evidence of hearths or furnaces are less easy to identify since a hearth might have been used for any type of metalworking. The debris of metalworking often contains the crucibles used for refining or melting precious metals. Crucible fragments with silver residues have been found in Foster Lane in the City of London on a site almost opposite the site of Goldsmiths' Hall. In Canterbury, at Longmarket, the badly disturbed remains of a building were found in the rear of a property fronting onto Burgate, which is known from rentals to have been occupied by Theoric the Goldsmith in c.1200. An extensive deposit of burnt clay flooring, together with traces of ovens and furnaces as well as metalworking debris including many crucible fragments, strongly suggests the presence of a metalworking workshop, which may have belonged to Theoric.

Evidence of a goldsmith, who also worked as an enameller at the beginning of the fourteenth century, was found during excavations to the north of the basilica of Saint-Denis, near Paris.

27 Jewish goldsmiths from an Old Testament picture book produced in northern Italy, probably Padua, c.1400. It represents the story from the Book of Exodus of Bezalehel and Oliab making candlesticks and other liturgical objects for use in the tabernacle.

There were fragments of refractory ceramics attributable to a portable oven, as well as crucibles whose residues contained tin, lead and silver. There were fragments of different coloured glass destined to be powdered, a piece of translucent agate used as a burnisher, and rock crystal 'doublets', or imitations of precious stones. This archaeological find shows a diversity of craftsmens' activities – the assembly of glass for enamelling, the melting of silver in crucibles, and the repair of objects – which contrasts with the simpler definition of activities often presented by the regulations of the craft guilds.

Of the medieval craftsmen, the goldsmith undertook many more careful manual and instrumental operations than most. Patience and precision were needed in working out the design, preparing materials and tools and executing the work, while an understanding and experience of the materials was essential to achieve the required effect. The techniques of working gold and silver included raising, sinking and embossing, but the two basic ones were forging it with a hammer or casting it. The different natures of the two metals led to different methods of working. Pure gold is exceptionally malleable and can be beaten into very thin leaf. Silver is less malleable than gold and after prolonged hammering needs annealing (reheating gently and then cooling). Sometimes the proportion of gold and silver in the alloyed metal was varied in order to exploit these qualities. Generally, most vessels and dishes were forged while jewellery and decorative details were cast. The scenes of the goldsmith working that are illustrated generally show him working with the hammer and the anvil. On some of the chalices, bowls and cups of silver the marks of hammering can be clearly seen.

Molten gold and silver was sometimes cast directly onto objects or parts of objects. Here the goldsmith had often to possess the modelling qualities of a sculptor. The casting process involved is called the lost wax, or 'cire perdue', technique. For instance, Theophilus describes the manufacture of the handles for the chalice by forming the handles in wax and sculpting on them decoration in the form of dragons, animals or birds. A little finger of wax called the sprue is left at the top. The wax is then covered in kneaded clay so that all the hollows of the moulding are filled. The mould is warmed so that the wax runs out through the holes created by the sprues. The molten silver is then poured into the moulds through the same holes. The whole then cools, the moulds are broken and the handles removed.

Where it was necessary to produce the same metal objects in large numbers, moulds of fine grained stone or metal were used. These could either be open moulds or moulds made in several pieces (piece-moulds). It is often impossible to say from the moulds that survive in museums or are found on excavations which metals were cast in them. A finely carved mould showing the Massacre of the Innocents survives 29 in Norwich Castle Museum but it may not necessarily have been used for precious metal.

Metal 'dies' were sometimes made of copper alloy. These enabled motifs to be reproduced in considerable numbers by placing a sheet of the metal over the die, and then a piece of lead over that and striking it with a hammer. A die piece from London shows a variety of designs, some of which overlap each other showing that it was 28 in repeated use. Small three dimensional motifs, such as the finials for spoons, were made in moulds and occasionally examples are found of the use of the same mould for decorative features on different objects. For instance the finial of one set of spoons made in 1536/7 is made from the same model or mould as a similar 43, 44 figure on the crozier of Bishop Fox commissioned in about 1501. This shows that the moulds could have remained in goldsmiths' workshops for considerable periods.

The different parts of jewellery or silver objects were riveted or soldered. Two types of solder were used, either a lead tin solder with a melting point below 250°C or a hard solder of copper alloyed with silver or of copper alloyed with gold which had a melting point of over 700°C.

Gold and silver were decorated by techniques such as embossing, or repoussé (work produced by working the metal from the back), or chasing

28 A mid-fourteenth-century copper-alloy goldsmith's mould, found in London. This would have been used for producing brooches and dress fittings in the form of birds, faces, a squirrel and the wheel of fortune. Such thin pieces of metal would have been sewn onto garments to catch the light when the wearer moved.

29 The high and delicate relief of the this mid-thirteenth-century stone mould found in Norwich may suggest that it was used to cast precious metal. It may have been used in the production of a shrine, possibly for a child martyr.

30 (raising up the metal from the front), or engraving (where the metal was gouged out). Punched surface decoration on gold ranged from rather crude small circles to the very fine pounced lines 53, 54 of dots that occur, for instance, on the Royal Gold Cup.

The surface of goldsmiths' work was given contrast and colour in a number of ways either by the use of niello, stones or enamel. Niello was 17 a sulphide of copper or silver fired onto an engraved metal surface that gave a matt black surface contrasting with the bright silver or gold around it. Decoration with enamel was much favoured in the Middle Ages since it gave a colourful contrast with the precious metal. Enamel is essentially glass which, when heated to its melting point, bonds to the metal with which it is in contact. It is only stable when the glass and the metal are compatible. The difference between the various enamelling techniques lies mainly in the way in which

the different metal surfaces were prepared to contain the enamel. There are a number of techniques for the application of the enamel to the metal. The enamel is contained within metal strips or boundaries, in which case it may be *cloisonné*, filigree, *champlevé*, or *basse-taille*. In *champlevé* enamelling the design was gouged 12 from the surface of the metal and the hollows were filled with enamel, often with several colours in a compartment. This technique was most frequently used on copper alloy since it required a considerable thickness of metal. *Busse-taille*, or translucent enamel, was a development 52, 68 of the late thirteenth century: a design in low relief was engraved in the groundplate of gold or silver. Differences in tone and modelling 53, 54 could be achieved by changes in the depth of the engraving and also in the thickness of the enamel. Secondly, the technique may exploit the property of enamel of fusing to the metal. This includes *ronde bosse* and painted enamel. Enamel

30 The Middleham Jewel is a rare gold pendant set with a sapphire, *c.*1450. It is engraved on one side with the Trinity and on the other with the Nativity. Found at Middleham, Yorkshire.

en ronde bosse was a technique of enamelling the surface of figures or objects which were in high relief or sometimes in the round. In this technique, developed in the fourteenth century, the enamel was held in place by roughening the surface of the gold or silver. A good example is 34 the Dunstable Swan Jewel.

The names of the enamelling techniques are expressed in French and certainly Paris was the leading centre of enamelling in northern Europe. Sometimes goldsmiths did their own enamelling but in a major centre such as Paris there were specialised enamellers. Among those recorded in 1292 was a Richard, 'esmailleur de Londres'. The 1370 Ordinances of the London Goldsmiths bracket enamellers and engravers together because they were both expected to return to the customer the same weight in gold and silver they had been given initially. Occasionally a gold object might be decorated with enamel and the enamelled surface decorated with gold leaf. An example is the heart- 37 shaped brooch from Fishpool.

In fact, the surfaces of many objects may be covered with gold leaf, no matter what they are made of — wood, ivory, metal — if a suitable adhesive such as size is used to hold the leaf in place. The making of gold leaf was a slow process. The goldsmith hammered the gold, often in the form of coin, into foil and beat it with a variety of hammers between parchment leaves until the required thinness was reached. The usual method of gilding silver and copper alloy was mercury gilding or fire gilding. In this, the object was cleaned and an amalgam of gold and mercury, made by dropping gold leaf or filings into boiling mercury, which was then cooled, was applied to the parts to be gilded. The object was then heated, causing the mercury to evaporate and leaving behind a gold layer ready for burnishing. Silvering was carried out by a similar means. The final effect of much medieval goldsmiths' work was the contrast between the colour of the stones or enamel with the shining surface of silver or gold.

31 A gold thirteenth-century ring brooch, either French or English, set alternately with red rubies and blue sapphires *en cabochon* and with punched decoration between them. On the back is an inscription of love.

32 Gold brooch set alternately with three chalcedony cameos and three cabochon rubies. The cameos probably date from the mid thirteenth century but the brooch was more likely to have been made *c.*1320–40. Found at Oxwich Castle in Wales.

33 *Opposite* Silver-gilt casket engraved with traceried arches and the arms of England and France. Made by a goldsmith in either England (perhaps London) or France (perhaps Paris), *c*.1300.

34 The Dunstable Swan Jewel, an example of opaque white enamel over gold, probably made by a London goldsmith, *c*.1400.

5 THE PRODUCT

The regulations for the Munich goldsmiths, written in the second half of the fourteenth century, begin with the words: 'the goldsmith makes belts, chains, and larger things'. The rhyme in the *Book of Trades* of Jost Amman, written in 1568, is illustrated and translated in Fig.35. Although this was written after the Reformation, it is clear that even during the Middle Ages most of what the goldsmith produced were secular objects such as silver bowls, beakers, cups, fittings for knives and horns, belts, and silver and gold rings. If a goldsmith used a symbol of his craft on his personal seal it was usually a brooch or covered cup. The description of the goldsmiths on the bridge over the Seine at Paris already quoted from Jean de Garlande stresses the secular side of their production (see p.11). Although today church treasuries and museum cases show chalices, reliquaries and crucifixes this can give a misleading impression of the output of the medieval goldsmith.

The production of everyday objects that formed the staple trade of the goldsmith can be illustrated by two hoards of goldsmiths' work. The first was found at the castle of Chalcis on the island of Euboea in Greece and consists of a series of fourteenth-century silver belt fittings and a chain that would have been used for personal adornment. It is not known exactly where they were made but they might well have come from the less fine Venetian workshops. The form of the buckles and belt ends and the use of openwork tracery and grotesque animals reflect the decorative motifs of northern Europe, possibly suggesting that the Venetian goldsmiths were influenced by northern decoration.

The second hoard was found at Fishpool in Nottinghamshire, England, with a large number of gold coins giving the date of deposition as 1464. The hoard is composed of a brooch, locket, roundel, cross, four rings and a chain. It is entirely of gold and was worth around £400 at the time of burial. It is likely that the only person who could have afforded such a sum would have

35 *Right* An engraving of the goldsmith at work together with a rhyme describing his products, from Jost Amman's *Book of Trades* written in 1568. The rhyme translates: I, the goldsmith make valuable things/ seals and golden signet rings/ costly pendants and jewels/ set with precious stones/ gold chains, necklaces, bracelets/goblets and beakers/also silver dishes and bowls/for whoever is willing to pay me.

36 *Below* A group of silver belt fittings, belt plates and applied plaques for belts, found in a hoard in the nineteenth century at the castle of Chalcis, Euboea (Greece). They range in date from the fourteenth century to the mid fifteenth century.

Der Goldtschmid.

Ich Goldtschmid mach köstliche ding/
Sigel vnd gülden petschafft Ring/
Köstlich gehcng vnd Kleinot rein
Versetzet mit Edlem gestein/
Güldin Ketten/Halß vnd Arm band/
Scheuren vnd Becher mancher hand/
Auch von Silber Schüssel vnd Schaln/
Wer mirs gutwillig thut bezaln.
 H ij   Der

37 Part of the hoard of gold jewellery buried at Fishpool, Nottinghamshire, early in 1464. The jewellery is elaborately decorated with black-letter inscriptions, engraved flowers and foliage and enamelling. The roundel has a central sapphire surrounded by white enamel beads on stalks; this may have been imported or possibly made in England by a goldsmith working in a Continental style.

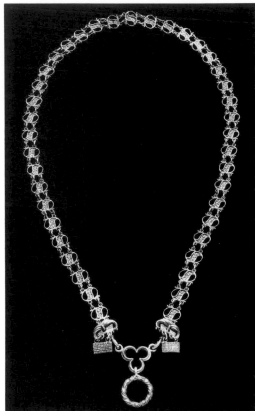

38 *Left* A secular silver cup, *c.*1400–50, long preserved as a chalice at the parish church of Lacock, Wiltshire (now on loan to the British Museum).

39 *Above* Silver collar of SS consisting of a chain of forty-one letters of S meeting in an ornamental arrangement of buckles and links ending in a fluted ring. It probably dates from the middle of the reign of Henry VI, *c.*1440, and may have been made by a London goldsmith.

40 Silver-gilt drinking cup with a curved handle. French or German, fifteenth century. Gold, silver and silver gilt were the most prized materials for use on the table.

been a rich merchant or a noble involved in the War of the Roses. The elaborate decoration with black-letter inscriptions, roses and foliage is typical of the fine jewellery produced in the mid fifteenth century, and may well be the sort of work produced by a goldsmith such as Edmund Shaa.

A silver collar found in the Thames probably dates from a few years earlier than the hoard, perhaps around 1440. It is made of forty-one 39 linked letters of S and is the distinctive livery of the royal house of Lancaster, and was granted by all three Lancastrian kings (Henrys IV, V and VI) to those they wished to honour. The collar illustrates the sort of silver chain or collar which would have been granted to someone below the rank of knight, perhaps an ambassador. Some collars were, in contrast, very expensive since they were heavy with gold and stones. For instance in 1408 Henry IV paid the London

goldsmith Drew Barantyn £550 for a collar of gold garnished with precious stones for his, the King's, own use.

The goblets and platters and bowls mentioned, for example, by Jost Amman represent the silver plate that was constantly in demand. Most secular plate was used for the serving of 40, 41 wine or ale, at the table or for display. One of the finest existing pieces of fifteenth-century silver is the Lacock cup which has survived as a chalice 38 in a Wiltshire parish church but which originally would have graced a secular dining table. The fine contrast between the smooth curves of silver and the bands of gilding on the base and finial, and the moulded cresting around the stem and lid, gives it a restrained elegance.

For articles of silver plate it is possible to calculate the relationship between the value of the metal and the cost of the workmanship. For example, among the plate presented by the City

41 *Left* Hexagonal silver jug. Probably made in Burgundy, late fourteenth century. It was a common vessel of its time, often seen in paintings of feasts. Its only decoration is the beading around the base, lid and top and the dragon's head at the end of the spout.

42 *Right* A nineteenth-century engraving by J. Skelton of the silver salt of Bishop Fox, made while he was Bishop of Durham, 1494–1501, and preserved in Corpus Christi College, Oxford. It is ornately decorated with his device of a pelican in its piety, and is mounted with crystal, pearls and enamel.

of London to the Black Prince, son of Edward III, on his return from Gascony in 1371 there are six chargers whose value in weight was £14.18s.9d. and which were worth £21.7s.2d., twelve hanaps or handled cups weighing £8.12s. and worth £12.7s.7d., and thirty salt cellars weighing £15.6s.2d. and worth £21.17s.8d. From these it would appear that the cost of manufacture may be set at half the value of the silver.

The thirty salt cellars given to the Black Prince would no doubt have been intended to be used among the guests at grand feasts. In front of the place of honour there would be placed a great or standing salt of much finer workmanship. This was one of the principal pieces of medieval domestic plate and emphasised the wealth and status of the owner as much as his position at the table. Unfortunately none of the salts mentioned in the accounts of the Black Prince survive, but at Corpus Christi College, Oxford, there is today the magnificent salt made

while Richard Fox was Bishop of Durham (1494–1501). Made of silver, it is ornately decorated, gilded and mounted with crystal, pearls and enamel. The salt is not marked so the goldsmith responsible is not known, but it is more likely that Fox would have commissioned it from a London goldsmith than one in Durham.

Silver spoons must have been a profitable and regular line in the production and sales of the goldsmith. Medieval silver spoons of the late fourteenth and fifteenth centuries have a characteristically pear-shaped bowl and the stems are often decorated with finials shaped in the form of acorns or diamond points. The most elaborate form of finial in the fifteenth century was the apostle finial, so called from the fact that sets were made showing the twelve Apostles and Christ. A sixteenth-century set of thirteen such spoons survives and from the marks on the spoons we know that they were made in London in 1536–7 but the goldsmith is unknown, since the makers' mark, which might be

43 Thirteen silver spoons with finials representing the twelve Apostles and the Virgin. They were made in London in 1536–7 by an unidentified goldsmith.

44 *Right* The final figure of St Andrew.

45 The Savernake horn was carved in the twelfth or thirteenth century out of elephant ivory; two silver bands were added in the mid fourteenth century. The lower shows a fox, hound and stag reserved against a translucent enamel background; the upper, from which most of the enamel has disappeared, shows a hound, stag and seated lion and illustrates how the silver surface was engraved to provide a pattern that would appear through the enamel and help to secure it.

46 *Right* A fifteenth-century silver-gilt spoon, probably made by a Flemish goldsmith, elaborately decorated with enamelled flowers and the inscription *ave maria*.

a sheaf of corn, is difficult to interpret precisely. The goldsmith did, however, make use of models for three of the finials for they had been used earlier for the figures on the crozier made for Richard Fox, before 1501 and which is now preserved at Corpus Christi College, Oxford. It is apparent that figure patterns and moulds were used over long periods by goldsmiths specialising in spoons since the figure of the Virgin on the 1536–7 set reappears on a later spoon dated to 1577–8.

Another example of secular objects made by goldsmiths are the silver or gold mounts used to decorate horns and baldrics (sword or bugle belts). An elaborately decorated gold-mounted hunting knife and hunting horn which has tassels of green silk was made in 1386 by John Bottesham of London, goldsmith, for Richard II. 45 The Savernake horn, which has richly enamelled fourteenth-century mounts of silver, was originally hung from a green baldric with silver mounts and gives some impression of this type of object. The silver mounts on the baldric are enamelled with Scottish heraldry and it may well be that these mounts are unusual survivals of the art of the Scottish medieval goldsmith.

Goldsmiths were also generally the makers of seals from the twelfth century onwards and many seal engravers were known as goldsmiths. Some seals were made of silver, such as the very 47 fine equestrian seal of Robert Fitzwalter which shows him galloping across the seal with a dragon beneath him. William de Keyles, a London goldsmith, made a Great Seal in silver and a privy seal in gold for Margaret, Queen of Edward I, in 1299. Neither of the seals survive today but there are impressions of both sides of 48 the Great Seal, one of which shows Queen Margaret standing and the other the arms of England hanging from a tree. Not all the seals that the goldsmiths cut were of precious metal, for Adam de Thorp, a London goldsmith, was paid £1.13s.4d. in 1390 for engraving a brass seal with the King's arms.

That goldsmiths produced gold and silver plate for the Church has already been discussed. The service of the Mass needed plate in the form of chalices and patens, cruets, pyxes, paxes and

47 The silver seal matrix of Robert Fitzwalter (d.1235). The effect of this fine equestrian figure and inscription has been achieved by the combination of engraving tools and punches. It is shown here in reverse.

48 Impressions of the obverse and reverse of the silver Great Seal of Margaret, second Queen of Edward I, made in 1299 by the London goldsmith William de Keyles.

49 A silver-gilt crozier attributed to a goldsmith of the school of Hugo d'Oignies, mid thirteenth century. It is decorated with naturalistic foliage and a dragon in gilt bronze.

50 *Opposite* Silver chalice made by an English goldsmith in the mid thirteenth century.

monstrances. Some chalices were gold and St Paul's Cathedral in London possessed several in 1245. However, most of the surviving medieval 50 chalices are silver. An example of a complete late medieval altar service is that commissioned by the Spanish nobleman, Don Pedro Fernandez de Velasco (1399–1469/70) from a Spanish goldsmith. It consists of chalice and paten, altar 51 crucifix, ciborium, candlesticks and processional cross, and was given to the Hospital de la Vera Cruz in Medina da Pomar, near Burgos, in about 1455.

Other liturgical practices created a demand for goldsmiths' work, such as crosses, croziers, 52 altarpieces, rings, shrines and reliquaries. Croziers, for instance, provided plentiful opportunities for the goldsmith to show his ability, as can be seen from the thirteenth-century crozier 49 attributed to Hugo d'Oignies and from the elaborate crozier for the Abbot of Bury St Edmunds for which a contract was drawn up in 1430. Rings, particularly the very elaborate rings known as pontifical rings which were worn by archbishops at the most important ceremonies, were another opportunity for displaying skill. The ring made for Walter de Gray, the Archbishop of York who died in 1255, is preserved at the treasury of York Minster, and is one of the finest examples.

Gifts between members of the royal families of medieval Europe led to the creation of fine pieces of goldsmiths' work. Gold plate has rarely survived from the Middle Ages. One of the most sumptuous pieces that has is the Royal Gold Cup of the kings of England and France, now preserved in the British Museum. Although the Cup does not present its original 53, 54 appearance since its stem has been heightened by the addition of two bands, and the crown of pearls and finial is missing from the cover, it is a remarkable example of the highest class of French, probably Parisian, goldsmiths' work from the late fourteenth century (it was probably produced in the 1380s). It is decorated with translucent enamel whose red, blue, yellow, dark brown and grey colours are reflected by the underlying gold. The enamel has been let into shallow troughs carved in the gold and the amount of light reflected back from the gold

51 Cross, chalice and candlesticks from an altar set made *c.*1455 by a Spanish goldsmith and given to a hospital. The arms of Don Pedro Fernandez de Velasco, who commissioned the set and was the founder of the hospital, are enamelled on many of the pieces.

52 *Opposite* This silver-gilt crucifix with translucent enamels was probably made by Peter Gallicus, a Sienese goldsmith in the service of Charles I of Hungary in the 1330s. It shows the arms of Hungary and the Hedervari family who probably commissioned it.

through the enamel is controlled by the depth of the trough and by this means the goldsmith can produce subtle variations of luminosity. The enamelled scenes tell the story of St Agnes. The Cup first appears in inventories as a gift from Jean, Duke of Berry, to the French King Charles VI in 1391. Since there is no evidence that the Duke had an especial veneration for St Agnes, it seems likely that he had commissioned it from a goldsmith as a gift to Charles V, his brother, who was born on St Agnes day (21 January). For some reason that gift was never made or possibly the Cup was never finished before the death of Charles V in 1380 and thus remained in the possession of the Duke who gave it to his nephew about ten years later.

Crowns were among the most important objects that a royal goldsmith might be required to make. The London goldsmith, Thomas Frowyck, made a golden crown in 1303 for Queen Margaret – and had difficulty in getting his bill paid (see p.67). One royal crown was sent 55 to Bavaria as part of the dowry of Blanche, daughter of Henry IV of England, who married Ludwig III of Bavaria in 1401. The crown was not made specifically for that occasion since it appears in a list of jewels and silver plate two years earlier, and it is likely, though not certain, that it may have belonged to Anne of Bohemia, the first Queen of Richard II. It may have been brought from Bohemia by Anne when she came to London to marry Richard in 1382, but the style of the enamel and the setting of the stones have led it to be attributed to either Paris or Venice. The difficulty of assigning this work to a particular country illustrates well the problem of understanding which medieval goldsmiths produced particular works of such high quality.

One of the most remarkable gifts to survive is the Little Golden Horse (Goldene Rössel) 57 preserved at Altötting in Bavaria. This was given to Charles VI, King of France, by his wife Isabella of Bavaria on New Year's Day 1404. The Madonna sits with the Christ Child under a canopy of jewelled flowers. Two angels hold a crown over her head. At her feet sit the two St Johns – the Baptist (with lamb) and the Evangelist (with chalice). Kneeling before the

53 *Left* The Royal Gold Cup of the Kings of England and France with enamelled scenes from the life of St Agnes. Probably made by a Parisian goldsmith shortly before 1380.

54 *Above* Detail from the lid of the Royal Gold Cup showing Procopius offering St Agnes jewels from a box. She refused his advances declaring that she was married to Christ.

55 *Opposite* The crown given as part of the marriage dowry of Blanche, daughter of Henry IV of England, who married Ludwig III of Bavaria in 1401. One of the finest achievements of the Gothic goldsmith, it is of gold set with sapphires, rubies, diamonds and pearls and is decorated with enamelling.

56 The effigy of Richard Beauchamp, Earl of Warwick, on his tomb at St Mary's Church, Warwick. The contract was drawn up in 1449, and the gilding was carried out by Bartholomew Lambespringe, a London goldsmith.

Madonna are the King in prayer and a page who holds the King's helmet. Beneath a groom tends the 'little horse' itself, made of pure gold but enamelled white. The use of enamel to represent the pure whiteness of this horse with its golden harness is one of the marvels of the medieval goldsmith.

Finally, the goldsmiths' work sometimes assisted in the commemoration of the dead. Most funeral effigies in the Middle Ages were carved from either wood or stone. Effigies of metal were normally reserved for royalty or members of the higher aristocracy. For example, a tomb for which there is direct evidence of the involvement of a goldsmith is that erected to the memory of Richard Beauchamp, Earl of Warwick, at the church of St Mary's, Warwick. This tomb also shows how the work of a number of craftsmen was organised by contract by the executors. The tomb chest was of Purbeck marble supplied by John Bord of Corfe Castle, Dorset, according to a 'portraiture' or drawing delivered to him in 1447. In the niches on the side of the tomb are a series of copper images of aristocratic relatives of the Earl. These were cast in 1452 by William Austen, a bronze founder of London, and were gilded by Bartholomew Lambespringe, a Dutchman and a goldsmith of

London. It is interesting to note that Austen was paid 13s.4d. for each image while Lambespringe was paid £40 for thirty-two images exclusive of the cost of the gold that he used 'for polishing, and gilding and for making the visages and hands and all the other bares of the images, in most quick and fair wise'. The life-size copper effigy of the Earl on the top of the tomb in the centre of the Chapel was produced by four London craftsmen. These were Roger Webbe, a barber surgeon, William Austen, the bronze founder, John Massingham, a wood carver and Bartholomew Lambespringe, the goldsmith. The cast copper effigy is made in seven pieces from a soft alloy with a copper content as high as 84 per cent. This softness of the metal explains the importance of the role of the goldsmith in this group of craftsmen for it was due to his work in engraving, polishing and gilding that the final effect of the sculpture was produced. The surface treatment of this effigy, in particular the detail of the armour and the physical features of the Earl, make it one of the most remarkable and realistic pieces of sculpture in England in the fifteenth century. Much of the detail was due to Webb, Austen and Massingham. The gilding, literally the finishing touch, was the work of a London goldsmith.

57 The Little Golden Horse (Goldene Rössel). This was a New Year's present from Isabel of Bavaria to her husband Charles VI in 1404. The name comes from the little horse, tended by the groom underneath the main scene. The horse is made of pure gold but is enamelled white.

6 ORGANISATION OF THE CRAFT

The activities of the medieval goldsmiths as craftsmen were controlled by a guild. Guilds were associations of people who shared a particular religious devotion (for instance, to a particular saint) or groups of leading citizens in a town, sometimes, but not always, craftsmen. How did the guild control the activities of the craftsmen and the quality of the precious metals with which they worked? What was the social life of the guild? What was the influence of migrant goldsmiths on the established goldsmiths in a town? These are the questions that will be considered in this chapter.

The patron saint of the English goldsmiths was St Dunstan while most of the continental guilds adopted St Eligius as their patron. St Dunstan was a Benedictine monk who was responsible for many of the monastic reforms in England in the tenth century and who later became Archbishop of Canterbury (960–88). According to popular legend, he was a skilful metalworker and bell founder, played the harp and loved the music of the human voice. In an illumination of the fourteenth century he is shown working at his anvil. The angelic figure playing the harp is probably a reminder of the legend that one day when St Dunstan was at his work, his harp, hanging against the wall, began to play of its own accord. Another legend records that he tweaked the nose of the Devil

with his goldsmiths tongs – a story that inspired the embroidered scene of St Dunstan on the Stonyhurst Chasuble. 59, back cover

His continental counterpart, St Eligius (or Eloi), was Bishop of Noyon and Tournai (641–60). He had a great talent for engraving and silversmithing which he had developed in his work at the mints of Limoges and Marseilles. He is shown in a number of paintings, either working in his shop and visited by two strangers, one of whom is Christ, or as a goldsmith hammering at the gold jewel-studded covering of a saddle which legend records he was asked to make for the Merovingian King Clotaire II. front cover, 21 contents page, 60

The guilds of goldsmiths who adopted St Dunstan and St Eligius as their patron saints were associations which regulated the trade and craft, including the quality of the product, the manner of producing it, the competence of the craftsmen and the apprenticeship of new members. All across Europe goldsmiths formed guilds. There was one in existence in Paris in the mid thirteenth century and one in Montpellier by the end of that century. In London in the thirteenth century there was a fraternity of St Dunstan which had wardens and was an organisation capable of managing property. This may well have been a successor body to the guild fined £120 in 1179–80

58

58 *Right* This illustration of St Dunstan shows the saint working at his anvil. The angel playing the harp probably refers to the legend that once when St Dunstan was at work, his harp, hanging against the wall, began to play of its own accord.

59 *Opposite* St Dunstan, the patron saint of goldsmiths, in his workshop. This detail from the Stonyhurst Chasuble, *c*.1470, shows the saint tweaking the nose of the Devil; on the bench beside him stands a chalice, bowl and covered cup with writhen decoration.

(see p.11). In London in the fourteenth century the major crafts were controlled by companies with a royal charter. These later became known as livery companies – a term derived from the special dress, or livery, which their full members wore on special occasions. All companies and guilds played a much greater role than a simple economic one or purely regulatory one. Their purposes included a number of ceremonial functions such as conducting the burial of members, commemorating past members or providing conviviality for the living.

The regulation of working in gold and silver was of particular importance to medieval kings who had a duty to maintain a supply of coin sufficient to meet the needs of the subjects and to ensure that the silver and gold coins supplied were of the correct weight and purity. The supply of precious metal, the coinage and the purity of precious metal objects were all connected. Goldsmiths were forbidden to produce silver wares of poorer quality than coinage. The association of the standards of coinage with the making and selling of gold and silver objects formed the background to the working lives of all the important and middle-ranking London goldsmiths.

The king needed the services of goldsmiths in order to bring about monetary reform. For instance, English coins were often more valuable than the foreign coins circulated in England, and this lead to the deterioration of the quality of the coinage. This was corrected in the thirteenth century by the calling in of the coin and its recoining. In 1279 a major reform of coinage took place and the royal mint was moved from the Old Change to the Tower of London. The main force behind these reforms was the goldsmith Gregory Rokesle, who was not only Mayor of London but also, from 1279 to 1291, Warden of the Tower Mint and Keeper of the Exchange. (The chief officers in the Mint and the Exchange were often goldsmiths as we have seen from the career of Sir Edmund Shaa and his nephew.) The Trial of the Pyx, a ceremony involving random testing of coins against trial plates (see p.60), required goldsmiths to act as judges.

67

60 St Eligius represented as a goldsmith in a painting attributed to Taddeo Gaddi and dating to the first half of the fourteenth century. He works at the gold covering of a saddle in accordance with the legend that he was commissioned to make a gold saddle studded with jewels for Clotaire II.

The king also needed the whole organisation of the goldsmiths' craft to supervise the manufacture of gold and silver objects. In 1300 the responsibility of carrying out the rules and the practice of the manufacture of gold and silver plate was imposed on the leading goldsmiths. One of the most important of these rules was that no gold or silver wares were to be made below the Paris standard for gold (19.2 carats) and for silver (sterling, 92.5 per cent). Silver wares had to be assayed by the wardens and marked with a leopard's head. The choice of the leopard's head probably reflected the leopards that featured on the royal arms. Gold had to be assayed by the wardens who visited each shop. Provincial towns had to observe the rules laid down in the statute of 1300. This statute was reinforced by the royal charter which the goldsmiths obtained in 1327. They were to elect good men skilled in the craft who were to see that the craft was properly managed. Goldsmiths' wares were not to be sold to merchants for export, and goldsmiths' shops were to be confined to Cheapside, the street in London leading east from St Paul's, in order that they could be properly surveyed.

The fourteenth century saw an increase in the importance and effective organisation of the Goldsmiths' Company. The success of the company in the fifteenth century is shown by its adoption of heraldic arms. The arms also occur on the memorial brasses of goldsmiths, for example, the brass of a goldsmith member of the Latham family buried in Upminster church in Essex. The device which appears on arms or seals varies. London goldsmiths certainly had a corporate seal although no impression of it appears to have survived. Some seals show products or tools, such as the seal of the goldsmiths of Cologne which depicts on a shield a gem ring between three covered cups with three crowns across the top. The seal of the goldsmiths of Brunswick depicts an anvil with a vessel above it. Others show St Eligius either working at the anvil, as on the seals of Vienna or Breslau, or as a bishop holding a chalice and hammer, as in that of Kashau (Kosice).

The relationship between the goldsmiths of a capital city and those in the lesser towns of a

61 *Above* Shield from a monumental brass showing the arms of the Goldsmiths' Company. From a church at Upminster, Essex, it probably comes from the tomb of a goldsmith.

62 *Below* A wax impression of 1396 of the seal of the company of goldsmiths of Cologne, showing their shield of arms.

63 *Top left* Impression of the seal of the Brunswick goldsmiths' guild, showing an anvil, bowl and hammer; second half of the fourteenth century. *Top right* Drawing of the seal of the Vienna goldsmiths' guild showing St Eligius making a chalice; *c.*1367. *Bottom left* Drawing of the seal of the goldsmiths of Breslau showing St Eligius at work; mid fifteenth century. *Bottom right* The face of the seal matrix of the goldsmiths of Kashau, Czechoslovakia, showing St Eligius with a hammer and chalice; engraved in 1476.

64 Bronze sheet with the names and the marks of the Ghent goldsmiths, 1454–81.

country was always likely to cause difficulties. For instance, in England in the fourteenth century there was a considerable growth of provincial goldsmiths. One such was Hugh le Seler who, in 1333, made a new seal for the bishopric of Durham at York; Hugh was probably part of a York family of goldsmiths. The control of provincial goldsmiths was an important matter for the London goldsmiths. The charter of 1327 repeated the order that provincial goldsmiths were to send two goldsmiths to London to familiarise themselves with the Londoners' punch for gold and the punch with the leopard's head with which to mark their work. This oversight of the provincial goldsmiths was certainly carried out for in 1328 the Wardens appointed an Oxford goldsmith to see that the London Ordinances were observed in Oxford, and they also appointed two goldsmiths in York to see that their ordinances were observed in the northern counties. The powers of the London goldsmiths over provincial goldsmiths were extended in 1372 so that they could visit fairs, such as Boston in Lincolnshire and Stourbridge in Worcestershire, to inspect and assay. In 1441 the Prior of Lewes sent the Wardens of the Goldsmiths' Company a parcel gilt nef (ship) used as an almsdish. Tests showed that nine of the turrets were stuffed with tin and lead, and so the ship was broken into pieces and returned to the Prior and the proceedings entered in the register of the company as evidence of the untruth of John Blemell, goldsmith of Lewes, who had made the ship. Presumably the Prior obtained subsequent direct satisfaction from the goldsmith.

In the fifteenth century there was a great change in the standard of gold purity and also in the marking arrangements. Since 1300, the minimum standard for wares of gold had been 19.2 carats. In 1478, it was lowered to 18 carats at which it was to remain until raised in 1576 to 22 carats. The change in the marking arrangements was no less dramatic. In 1478 an assayer was appointed and all gold and silver objects were to be brought to Goldsmiths' Hall in Foster Lane to be assayed and marked. The Wardens, however, continued their inspections in the London area and also at the fairs for any

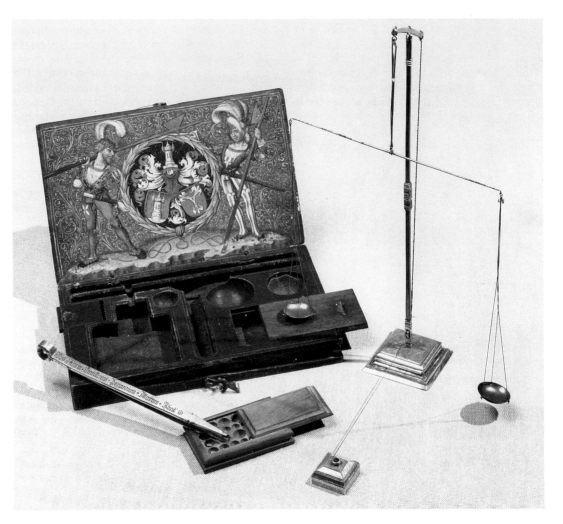

65 The Harsdorfer gold and gem scale, 1497. It was made of silver gilt, the balance beam of iron, and has a painted wooden case.

goldsmiths who did not comply. It is from 1478 that the phrase 'hall marking' occurs; previously it had been referred to as 'touch'. From that date, the mark or touch was changed from a leopard's head to a crowned leopard's head, and the goldsmiths were ordered to enforce its use.

Another new development was the institution in 1478 of a cycle of twenty-one date letters, from A to U (or V). After the cycle had been completed it started again with A in a different form. This idea of a cycle of date letters originated in 1427 in the French town of Montpellier as a result of a dispute between the

silversmiths and the royal minters over working sub-standard metal. The purpose of the date letter was to define the year and officers responsible for marking any piece of silver. The system was adopted in Paris in 1461, and subsequently in London in 1478.

Goldsmiths also had their own makers' marks and these were in use in London in the mid fourteenth century, although not much work was actually marked then. An Act of 1363 declared that every master goldsmith was to have his own mark known to those appointed by the king to oversee the goldsmiths' work, and that this should not be put on the work until it had been assayed. Makers' marks were omitted on many pieces of pre-1478 gold and silver as the frequent complaints make clear. In fact, it was not until the later fifteenth century in England that makers' marks were used extensively and even then it was often impossible to relate a particular mark to a known goldsmith. In Paris it is clear that by the middle of the fourteenth century each goldsmith had his own mark, and this may have been a long-established custom by that date. Although there were regulations that all pieces were to be marked by both the Wardens and the goldsmiths, this was not fully observed in the fourteenth century since many pieces are marked by only one or the other. The custom of regularly striking two marks, that of the town or Warden and the individual goldsmith, first occurred as a result of disputes in Montpellier in 1355 and subsequently became standard practice.

The accurate weighing of gold and gems was of the greatest importance to the medieval goldsmith. Fractional differences could bring great profit or heavy loss. In 1360 the London Company of Goldsmiths ordered that all goldsmiths' weights should be regularly sized and standardised, and in 1370 that they should be marked as well. The oldest surviving complete medieval gem and gold scale belonged to Hans Harsdorfer (d.1511) and is now in the Germanisches Nationalmuseum. It is a travelling scale which could be disassembled and carried with the weights in a painted wooden travelling case. Engraved on the base of the scale are the Harsdorfer and Nutzel arms since Harsdorfer married Margarethe, daughter of Gabriel Nutzel, the imperial mayor, in 1481. Harsdorfer owned silver mines in Bohemia and from 1496 to 1499 he was Chief Mint Master for Bohemia, which involved not only the minting of coins but also the supervision of mines such as those at Kuttenberg. He was one of those bankers who, by virtue of their special knowledge and fortune, was able to occupy an important position in the financial administration of the German empire.

How did the Company of Goldsmiths put into effect their regulations of quality, work conditions, apprenticeship and social life? Goldsmiths may or may not have been any different to other craftsmen in cheating their customers but the ordinances and records of the Goldsmiths' Company give some indication of the ways in which some customers were defrauded. (A simple fraud was experienced by the Prior of Lewes, see above.) The plating of base metal and passing it off as gold or silver was a repeated practice. Rings and buckles were made of a hollow section and passed off as solid. False stones, such as ones made of glass, were set in gold or real stones were set in copper or latten. Tinfoil was placed behind stones to give them greater lustre. The minutes of the Goldsmiths' Company indicate that fines for offences against quality occurred quite soon after the 1327 charter. For example, in 1334/5 Thomas de Algate was fined for setting glass in gold, counterfeiting a gemstone, and he repeated the offence the following year. As a result he was fined 6s.8d. and 5s.

The purity of gold was determined by a touchstone, a small piece of black fine-grained rock. This had to be sufficiently abrasive that a streak of gold was produced when a sample of gold was rubbed on the surface of the stone. This streak was then compared with alloys of known composition. Most touchstones consisted of sedimentary rock types such as tuffs, cherts and siltstones. The example illustrated

66 A goldsmith's touchstone engraved with his initials and merchant's mark. Flemish or Dutch, sixteenth century.

67 This ingot-shaped silver object in the Royal Mint has been identified as a trial plate. It probably dates from 1279.

is made of a fossiliferous limestone, perhaps Tournai marble. It is pierced at one end for suspension and at the other is shaped to a point on which is engraved in intaglio a merchant's mark within an oval frame. The statute of 1300 had required the Wardens to go from shop to shop to try the standard of the gold and for this they presumably used a touchstone. In 1469 the Wardens visited the house of Thomas a Wode 'finding there divers men working girdles, chalices, altar candlesticks and other plate ... whereof the Wardens made assay there and found it greatly faulty'. Wode was ordered to bring his wares to Goldsmiths' Hall for a fuller examination, probably by cupellation.

The ultimate standards for the goldsmiths, and those which provided the standard for the coinage of the realm, were set by the trial plates at the Royal Mint. The oldest surviving trial plate is silver, and the stamps of the coin dies on it date it to 1279. The oldest surviving gold plate is dated to 1477, again from the stamp of the coin. The goldsmiths played an essential part in the ceremony known as the Trial of the Pyx. The word 'pyx' refers to the box in which the plates or assay pieces were kept until the trial. The ceremony was carried out by a jury of Freemen of the Goldsmiths' Company: coins were presented to them and they selected random samples to be tested against the standard trial plates.

Sometimes a customer was defrauded over the weight of the goods. In 1458, Thomas Poole, a servant of the Earl of Wiltshire, took, on behalf of the Earl, some jewels to his old friend Edward Rawdon, a goldsmith, for melting down. Rawdon duly carried out the work and gave Poole a bill certifying the weight of the gold and the stones. Poole suspected that some knavery was afoot and brought his complaint before the Wardens. The melted down material was reweighed and it was found that Poole had been defrauded of 16 oz of gold. Rawdon was ordered to make up the deficiency and to pay Poole a further £16.16s.11d.

Goldsmiths had quite strict regulations concerning apprentices. These are usually concerned with the fees paid to the goldsmith or the guild or company, the length of time that the apprentice should serve, the discharge of an apprentice and the limits on the craft activities of apprentices. There is very little evidence on the manner of instruction of apprentices, or on the level of competence required of the apprentice at the end of his term. In London, for instance, no apprentice was to be taken for a term shorter than seven years, unless apprenticed to his own father; no goldsmith could take an apprentice without the Wardens knowing and approving; and finally, the apprentice had to pay a premium. The requirement that an apprentice produce a masterpiece before finally qualifying did not apply in England as it did in many continental guilds, and it is only in the sixteenth century that there is mention of the masterpiece in connection with the London crafts. Among the German and French guilds the masterpiece was important mainly as a device for excluding new members. The masterpiece was often so costly or elaborate that the ordinary journeyman could not afford either the money or time.

Nearly all goldsmiths were men, and women played only a very subsidiary part in the trade. Burnishing appears to have been a speciality of women since the ordinances of the Company specify that no member of the Company shall employ women burnishers who are married to men of other crafts. Occasionally women took over the business of their husband. For instance, Elizabeth Bryce succeeded her husband, Hugh, after his death in 1496, as can be gathered by the fact that she took on two apprentices in 1497. It is likely that goldsmiths' wives often manned and looked after the shop in their husbands' absence.

As for the social life of the goldsmiths as a body, St Dunstan's Day (19 May) was naturally the principal ceremonial day of the year for the London goldsmiths. The day was marked by a special bell ringing at the craft's expense in St Paul's. All goldsmiths' shops were shut, the Company assembled in full livery, the new Wardens were installed, the ordinances were read, business transacted and the whole day rounded off with refreshments or a feast that was to be attended by all members of the fraternity. The actual food served at the annual

68 Silver-gilt ewer decorated with translucent and opaque enamel. On the upper part, there are six scenes of games and on the lower, six scenes from an unidentified story. On the base there is a mark in the form of a *fleur-de-lis* indicating that it was made by a Parisian goldsmith, *c.*1320.

supper given by the four Wardens to their predecessors in 1497 is recorded. There were three courses. The first consisted of four dishes — venison, roast capon, pike and baked venison. The second was of cream of almonds, rabbit with chicken, turbot, pigeon and tarts. The third course was strawberries and cream. At the St Dunstan's Day entertainment in the following year thirty-two gallons of red wine, eight gallons of claret and two barrels of ale were drunk. It is not known how many came to this party but the traditional spice cakes and buns included 200 eggs, 12 lbs of butter, six bushels of flour, plus a firkin of ale to mix it and saffron, cloves, mace and pepper. Then, beside 30 lbs of the usual confits (sweetmeats) there were 2 lbs in the form of leopard's heads and brooches. In 1403 the Company spent heavily on its minstrelsy. It had bought clarions and pipes, a bombard, a cornemuse and a big and light shawm, all of which were instruments valuable enough to have a special chest bought for their safe keeping. It also paid its minstrels well since eight of them received 16s. in 1401. The fifteenth-century feasts of goldsmiths were lavish occasions of much merriment.

The feast was served and the minstrels played in Goldsmiths' Hall. The goldsmiths were the first London Company to have a Hall. The property was acquired in 1339 and a new Hall was built in 1366. Like a merchant's house or the house of a notable citizen, it contained a hall and kitchen, pantry and buttery, and two chambers. In 1382 a parlour was added which gave the Wardens a room in which they could be away from the ordinary members of the craft. The Hall was largely rebuilt in the second half of the fifteenth century, reflecting prosperity similar to that of Sir Edmund Shaa. The kitchen, pantry and buttery were rebuilt and in 1485 the goldsmiths Sir Edmund Shaa and Thomas Wood paid for the addition of a bay window, the latest fashion, to the Hall. Inside the Hall was a screen surmounted by a silver-gilt statue of St Dunstan, which was destroyed at the time of the Reformation. At the end of the Middle Ages the interior of the Hall was hung with tapestries which were commissioned by the goldsmiths from Flanders and which portrayed the history of St Dunstan. Among the costs of the tapestries was a payment of 10s. for translating the story from English into Dutch, implying that the designers were given a copy of the story to draw out the scenes. Tapestries were not the only furnishings, since there would have been tables and benches. In 1487 Elizabeth Philip, the daughter of John Walshe, a goldsmith of the Company who was six times Warden, gave for furnishing the Hall 'five fine cushions of verdone with the goldsmiths arms wrought in the middle of them, and the name of the said John Walshe wrought with red and white letters'. It may have been that these were for the Wardens' chairs. The impression given of the Hall at the end of the Middle Ages was of very comfortably furnished accommodation.

The richness and importance of the goldsmiths led to their taking a prominent part in City processions and pageants. One of the most [73] spectacular in London, recorded in the fourteenth century, was that for the Coronation of Richard II in 1377. At the upper end of Cheapside, a temporary castle, presumably of wood, was erected with four towers in which four beautiful young ladies, dressed in white, blew leaves of gold on the King's face and threw down before him counterfeit golden florins as he approached. They presented him and his nobles with cups of gold full of wine. On the top of the castle stood a golden angel holding a crown in his hand so that when the King came past, the angel bowed down and offered him the crown. The dress of the goldsmiths on such occasions could be very splendid. Six years after this Coronation there was a procession of the crafts to welcome the new Queen, Anne of Bohemia. (This may have been the moment at which the crown described earlier came to England). All the crafts were to be dressed parti-coloured in red and black. The goldsmiths decided to decorate the red of their dress with bars of silver-work and trefoils of silver, and the black part with fine knots of gold and silk. On their heads they wore hats covered with red and powdered with trefoils. It must have been a splendid sight.

While it is clear that many goldsmiths learnt their craft in their home town, practised it there,

69 The silver reliquary of the Corporale of Bolsena in the north transept of Orvieto Cathedral. In the form of a church facade, it was made in 1337 by the goldsmith Ugolino di Vieri and his associates from Siena.

prospered, and eventually died in the same place, others were restless and sought new opportunities in other towns or other countries. A goldsmith at St Albans in the twelfth century had advised the Danish king on coinage, and the pattern of the travelling goldsmith continues throughout the medieval period. London was a magnet for the English, as the career of Sir Edmund Shaa demonstrates. Paris likewise drew many from the French provinces but it also attracted many from the Low Countries and the areas across the Rhine. In the late fourteenth century a number of goldsmiths, such as Jean de Lille, Hans Karast, goldsmith to Louis Duke of Orleans, or Claus de Fribourg, came to Paris and prospered. Cologne acted as a magnet for German goldsmiths but also was notable for its goldsmiths appearing all over Europe from Spain to the Baltic. They were particularly numerous in France, the Netherlands, and Italy and in Venice there was a colony of goldsmiths from Cologne and other parts of Germany.

Foreign goldsmiths, apprenticed and qualified elsewhere in Europe, who came to England and practised their craft in the profitable London market, were a particular problem for the London goldsmiths and were increasingly common in London in the fifteenth century. They were usually referred to as Dutchmen but they came from a wide area of northern Europe, the Low Countries, Rhineland and other parts of Germany and the Baltic. Bartholomew Lambespringe who worked on the gilding of the tomb 56 of Richard Beauchamp was described as a Dutchman.

There was much rivalry between the goldsmiths in the City of London and goldsmiths from abroad who often settled in Southwark. Indeed late in the fifteenth century this rivalry was the cause of a competition between goldsmiths on the relative skill of English and German craftsmen. This arose in 1464 from an argument between Oliver Davy of London, and White Johnson, a German. The trial of skill took place at the Pope's Head Tavern in Cornhill. It was agreed that each should arrange for the making of four puncheons or dies to be made by a compatriot in a specified time. Two of the dies

were to be engraved and two to be embossed, and the two designs to be followed were a cat's face and a naked man. Davy brought four dies made by his apprentice Thomas Cottrell in the due time and Johnson came six weeks late with only the two engraved dies. The jury was composed of three English and three Dutch goldsmiths and they decided that Davy's were the better wrought. The loser had to pay Davy a crown and buy dinner at Goldsmiths' Hall for all those involved, including the Wardens of the Company.

There is not a great deal of evidence to show how goldsmiths arrived at a final design for a piece of work. Much, the production of rings, brooches or plate, would have been simple and repetitive. For more elaborate pieces, particularly when a contract was agreed, a drawing was sometimes mentioned. In the contract for the shrine of Gertrude of Nivelles in Belgium of 1272, the design was provided by Jakomon d'Anchin of the Abbey of Nivelles while the work was carried out by the goldsmiths, Colars de Douai and Jakemon de Nivelles. In the fifteenth century, there was a close relationship between engravers and goldsmiths in Germany. Much silver in Germany was engraved and the relationship between such engraved silver and the goldsmiths in the different centres of Germany has been carefully studied. The art of printing from engraved plates originated in the workshops of goldsmiths in south Germany in the 1430s, and engravers were predominantly goldsmiths until about 1470. The engravers known as the Master ES (active c.1450–67) and 13 Israhel von Meneckem (c.1445–1503) were both trained and practised as goldsmiths. The German graphic artists did much to spread the knowledge of different types of ornamental decoration, not only for plate, but also for jewellery. Albrecht Dürer (1471–1528), who was himself the son of a goldsmith, made several designs for jewellery, probably intended for his 70 brother to execute. These designs for jewels, composed of entwined and exotic dragons, dolphins, and mermaids, reflect, in their style, subject and subtle balance, the new influence of the Italian Renaissance.

70 Design for jewellery by Albrecht Dürer (1471–1528).

71 Silver chalice decorated with translucent enamels. Around the lower stem is an inscription indicating that it was made by the Sienese goldsmiths Tondino di Guerrino and Andrea Riguardi. It was probably produced in the 1320s. The exact division of work between the two goldsmiths is not certain but Tondino di Guerrino is likely to have been responsible for the chalice and Andrea Riguardi for the enamels.

7 CONTRACTS AND DISTRIBUTION

The material the medieval goldsmith designed, created and produced has now been covered, but how were these goods contracted and distributed to the markets of Europe? Since many objects involved expensive materials the goldsmith would not undertake their manufacture without a specific contract. On the other hand, the secular objects that made up the everyday production of the goldsmiths, the brooches, rings and silver plate, were made as stock and sold through shops. The ways of organising the different methods of production no doubt varied with time, place and the individual goldsmith in the Middle Ages.

Some specific contracts for the manufacture of particular objects survive. A contract drawn up in 1292 exists between Roger of Faringdon, goldsmith, and the Chapter of the church of St John at Beverley, for the new shrine for the relics of St John of Beverley, the local saint. The Chapter were to provide the necessary gold and silver which Roger was to refine. Roger was to supply his own quicksilver (mercury), charcoal and other materials for constructing the work. The shrine was to be 5 foot 6 inches long (1.6 m), 1 foot 6 inches broad (0.5 m) and of proportionate height; the design was to be architectural in style, adorned with columns and skilfully-worked statuettes, the number and size of which were to be decided by the Chapter. Should any of the work on the shrine not meet with the approval of the Chapter, on account of the material or workmanship, it was to be remade without extra charge. For his work Roger was to receive the weight in silver of each column or statue and no more. The shrine was completed only in 1308.

A more straightforward contract was drawn up in 1430 for a crozier to be made by John Horwelle, goldsmith, for William Curteys, the Abbot of Bury St Edmunds. It was an enormous crozier weighing 12 lbs 9¼ oz (over 4¼ kg) which was to be decorated with the Assumption of the Blessed Virgin on one side of the head, and the Salvation of the Virgin on the other. Around the head there were to be twelve tabernacles (niches) with the twelve Apostles in them and in the crook of the staff a tabernacle with the image of St Edmund. For all this work, made skilfully in gilded silver and by an agreed date, John was to receive £40. The manufacture of objects by contract may have seemed a more secure route to the making of money but it often involved the goldsmith in considerable initial outlay and occasionally a long wait for payment. For instance, Thomas Frowyk in 1303 made a golden crown for Queen Margaret, the second Queen of Edward I and had considerable difficulty in getting his bill paid. The crown was commissioned by three of the King's servants and when Thomas applied for payment they referred him to the King's Treasurer, who told him to make out his bill and leave it with John de Cheam, the receiver of the bills. However, John failed to take any notice of it and so when Thomas petitioned the King he was told that he might take his bill to the Clerk of the King's Exchange, who would then pay him in part before next Christmas. The perennial exasperation of the craftsman or businessman with bureaucracy comes out clearly in this account.

These contracts were with goldsmiths in London and they show how, very often, the rich commissions from the provinces went to London goldsmiths. Within capital cities there was a certain amount of concentration of goldsmiths in particular areas. As already mentioned, the chief centre of the goldsmiths' trade in Paris was the bridge over the Seine. There is evidence from other European towns for the grouping of goldsmiths in particular areas of the town. In Cologne they were grouped around the Cathedral, in Lübeck around the market place, and in Antwerp there was a 'silversmith's street' near the town hall. This concentration of goldsmiths arose from their living and working in the area in which their rich clients would gather and shop rather than from any restriction to one area or any idea that a particular street should be exclusive to goldsmiths. In Utrecht,

72 *Opposite* Silver chalice of the Franciscan Pope Nicolas IV, in the Treasury of the Church of St Francis, Assisi. This was made by the goldsmith Guccio di Mannaia of Siena between 1288 and 1292.

16, 19

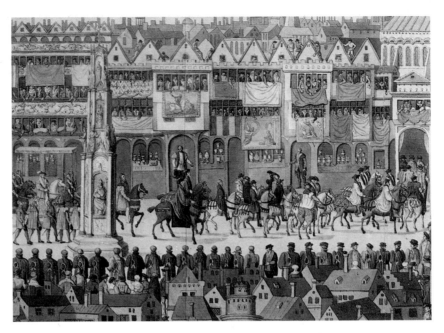

73 Goldsmiths' shops in Cheapside, London, shown in a painting of the coronation procession of Edward VI which took place in 1547.

for example, there were goldsmiths in many streets in different parts of the town.

Some goldsmiths worked for the courts of kings or rich noblemen. Their names are recorded in accounts and inventories. Some impression of such men is gained from documents that mention Jehan Duvivier, goldsmith to Charles V (1364–80) and Charles VI (1380–1422), kings of France, and Guillaume Arrode, who was goldsmith to Charles VI of France. Duvivier is recorded as working from 1364 to 1404. He supplied jewels and collars and was himself supplied with gold to make items such as a gold chain, a gold chaplet, a dagger of gold and other jewels. In August 1390 he was paid for repairing and cleaning the King's goblet. Jehan Duvivier did not work solely for Charles VI since he also worked for Charles's brother, Philip Duke of Burgundy (*d.*1404).

Guillaume Arrode was principally employed to repair and refurbish old plate and to supply new. The new plate was generally fashioned from old. In 1388 he made two new gilt plates, a new border for a third, and three gilt saucers from old silver supplied to him. The melting down of gold and silver was a frequent practice

particularly when new pieces were required. This explains the disappearance of so much medieval goldsmiths' work particularly of the plainer sort. Guillaume also made new plate of all kinds from the simplest to the most elaborate. In 1393 he carried out one of his most important works for the King. This was a plain gold covered shallow bowl decorated on foot and lid with nineteen gold roundels, ten enamelled with the arms of France and the other nine with the royal device of a white unicorn with a letter *b* enamelled in red on the shoulder. He made plate of silver and gold that the King gave away as presents, not only to other kings and ambassadors but also to his officials and advisers to secure their loyalty.

Louis, Duke of Anjou (*d.*1384), a brother of Charles V, was most interested in goldsmith's work. It was for him that Master Gusmin of Cologne, mentioned in Ghiberti's Commentaries, worked. Gusmin, according to Ghiberti, 'was perfect in his works, the equal of the ancient Greek sculptors, made heads marvellously well and every naked part: there was no failing in him save that his statues were a little short'. Ghiberti relates how Gusmin was broken-hearted when the Duke melted down his treasures, and seeing that all his labour had been in vain, prayed to God for his mercy and vowed to devote himself to his service. He gave away all his goods, and died in a hermitage in the mountains. Clearly some great goldsmiths were distressed at the loss of their creations, and not all ended their lives as successful and prosperous burghers.

The richest clients would no doubt arrange to have the goldsmiths call on them. The less important would have visited the goldsmiths in their shops. There are three types of evidence for such shops: written descriptions; inventories of goldsmiths' possessions; pictures of the shops. Goldsmiths' shops were usually to be 73 found in the goldsmiths' quarters and Cheapside was London's centre. One Venetian traveller in England in 1500 was astonished at the profusion and display of silver vessels in London:

In a single street leading to St Paul's there are fifty-two goldsmiths' shops so rich and full of silver vessels, great and small, that in all the shops in Milan, Rome, Venice and Florence put together I do not think there would be found so many of the magnificence that are to be seen in London. And these vessels are all either salt cellars or drinking cups or basins to hold water for the hands, for they eat off that fine tin which is little inferior to silver [pewter].

In the early fourteenth century the typical Cheapside shop would have been quite small – about 2 m wide and 3 m deep. It would have had a window opening onto the street with a doorway beside it. As the illustrations of the goldsmith at work show, the shop was often used as a workshop. The rear would have been used for storage space, probably using chests or coffers. Such a design was quite general across Europe. The shops often had solars or chambers above, used either for living or additional storage. In Cheapside in the second half of the fifteenth century, Thomas Wood built Goldsmith's Row; there were ten houses, fourteen shops all covered by a four-storied front adorned with allusive wild men of the wood riding on monstrous beasts. It is an early example of the rich and successful city magnate indulging in property speculation. The goldsmiths' shops of Cheapside can be seen in the mid-sixteenth-century painting of Edward vi's coronation procession through the city in 1547. This shows the products of the goldsmiths 73 exhibited in the fronts of shops which have been built with the elaboration and splendour that one would expect from the description of Goldsmith's Row.

Occasionally inventories of jewellers' shops have survived and these provide a cross-section of the stock held. In 1398 Walter Pynchon, a rich goldsmith and citizen of London, dwelling at Cornhill, and who was treacherously slain at Winchester, had his stock appraised by two other leading goldsmiths, Drew Barantyn and John Doblere. Its total value came to £600, and of this total the two most valuable objects were a royal chaplet and a royal nowche (brooch), both valued individually at £100. The stones in his possession were rubies (one valued at £40), diamonds and sapphires. There were forty-six rings and two small nowches of gold, a gold collar with a falcon, two nowches and a hart in gold (together valued at £11). The white hart was the personal badge of Richard ii and it is likely that this may have been made for sale to a supporter of the King. In addition there was a chaplet of pearls, over twenty gold rings, a gold seal, pearls, brooches and finally a mitre set with golden ornaments. The silver consisted of ewers, candlesticks, beakers, salt cellars, spoons and a pax (tablet with crucifixion kissed during the Mass). The total value of the silver only came to just over £15 indicating that the real value of his trade, when he was killed, lay in gold and precious stones.

One of the earliest manuscript illustrations of a goldsmith's shop is in a Genoese treatise of the second half of the fourteenth century on the Seven Vices. The goldsmith, standing behind a 74 table, concludes a bargain with a customer, using elaborate finger gestures. The customer's servant waits in the doorway while the goldsmith's assistant notes down the detail of the purchase in a book. Behind and on the table are spread the rich products of the goldsmith's art as well as gold and silver coins. It is these that encourage the vices of luxury and avarice as well as discord over their price.

Perhaps the finest and most informative depiction of a goldsmith's shop is the painting of

74 The interior of a goldsmith's shop from a Genoese treatise on the Seven Vices written between 1350–1400.

title page 1449 by the Flemish painter Petrus Christus. The simplest interpretation of the picture is that it shows the purchase of a betrothal or wedding ring. Whether a more complex explanation, which identifies the lady as the daughter of the goldsmith, is more likely must remain a matter of speculation.

The picture illustrates the varied products of the medieval goldsmith. On the shelf behind his head are two parcel-gilt, handled silver flagons with their plinths engraved with black-letter inscriptions; a lobed cup on feet formed as crouching lions represents silver plate, the usual product of the goldsmith. A wide silver-gilt buckle, that might well have fitted the belt lying across the counter, is pinned to the shelf, again a reminder of the importance of everyday objects to the craft of the goldsmith. Hanging from the shelf is a string of red amber and pale blue beads. Beneath is a piece of dark cloth to which are pinned three exquisite gold jewels, the type of aristocratic jewellery worn by the young noble in the picture. Beside are a pair of fossilised shark's teeth which would have been worn as protective charms or used to detect poison. The lowest shelf shows a series of curiosities – a mounted coconut cup, two matching pieces of rock crystal and dark stone, and a branch of red coral – all of which represent the rare and exotic. There is a cylindrical reliquary in rock crystal,

with a cover of twisted gadrooning, surmounted by a pelican in her piety. This may have been awaiting a suitable ecclesiastical customer. In front there are the unmounted stones – a packet of pearls and a packet of precious stones. Lastly, a box containing thirteen rings mounted on three rolls of parchment, the manufacture of which was no doubt one of the most reliable sources of income for the goldsmith.

The foreground of the picture shows the goldsmith at work – he holds the balance with a weight in it in his left hand and a ring in his right. No doubt it is the weight of the ring that determines the price. His open box of weights lies beside a pile of gold coins from Mainz, in Germany, England and the Duchy of Burgundy, evidence of the international exchange of gold coins and the interchange of goldsmiths between nations.

The close examination of the detail of engraving, filigree or the setting of stones is one of the great attractions and joys of the study of the art of the medieval goldsmith. Petrus Christus' painting shows a young couple in a goldsmith's shop, surrounded by and appreciating the products of a medieval goldsmith. That appreciation can be carried on today by examining the pieces displayed in treasuries and museums all over the world.

FURTHER READING

Techniques

THEOPHILUS,
De Diversis Artibus, ed. and trans. C. R. Dodwell, London, 1961. The best Latin text with English translation. Erhard Brepohl, *Theophilus Presbyter und die mittelalterliche Goldschmiedekunst*, Vienna, 1987, publishes the Latin text with a German translation. It is very useful for the technical drawings of tools and processes which bring the text to life.

England

MARIAN CAMPBELL,
'Gold, silver and precious stones' in *English Medieval Industries* ed. J. Blair and N. Ramsay, London, 1991, pp.107–66. The latest and most comprehensive survey of English medieval goldsmiths. It has a good bibliography.

T. REDDAWAY and L. WALKER,
A History of the Goldsmiths' Company 1327–1509, London, 1976. This considers the organisation of the craft in London, and contains much biographical detail on individual goldsmiths. For Sir Edmund Shaa see Anne F. Sutton and P. W. Hammond, *Coronation of Richard III*, London 1975, p.394 and B. Varley *The History of Stockport Grammar School*, Manchester, 1946.

English Romanesque Art 1066–1200, exhibition catalogue, London, 1984

Age of Chivalry: Art in Plantagenet England 1200–1400, exhibition catalogue, London, 1987.

France

R. W. LIGHTBOWN,
Secular Goldsmiths' Work in Medieval France, London, 1978.

E. TABURET-DELAHAYE,
L'Orfèvrerie Gothique au Musée de Cluny, Paris, 1989.

Les Fastes du Gothique, le siècle du Charles V, exhibition catalogue, Paris, 1981.

Germany

J. M. FRITZ,
Goldschmiedekunst der Gotik in Mitteleuropa, Munich, 1982. A wide-ranging, magisterial and excellently illustrated study.

Rhein und Maas, Kunst und Kultur, 800–1400, exhibition catalogue, Cologne, 1972.

Die Parler und der schöne stil 1350–1400, exhibition catalogue, Cologne, 1978.

Ornamenta Ecclesiae, Kunst und Kunstler der Romanik, exhibition catalogue, Cologne, 1985.

Gothic and Renaissance Art in Nuremberg, 1350–1550, exhibition catalogue, New York, 1986.

Italy

L'Oreficeria nella Firenze del quattrocento, exhibition catalogue, Florence, 1977.

European enamels

M. M. GAUTHIER,
Émaux du Moyen Age Occidental, Fribourg, 1972.

Coins

J. PORTEOUS,
Coins in history, London, 1969.

Jewellery

Seven Thousand Years of Jewellery, ed. Hugh Tait, London, 1986.

Detailed articles

C. C. OMAN,
'Goldsmiths at St Albans in the 12th and 13th centuries', in *Saint Albans and Herts Archit. and Archaeol. Trans.* 1932.

MARIAN CAMPBELL,
'English goldsmiths in the fifteenth century', in D. Williams *England in the fifteenth century*, 1987.

R. KENT LANCASTER,
'Artists, Suppliers, and Clerks ... to Henry III', in *J. Warburg and Courtauld Institutes* XXXV (1972).

D. T. MOORE and W. A. ODDY,
'Touchstones: some aspects of their nomenclature, petrography and provenance', in *Journal of Archaeological Science*, xii, 1985.

PHOTOGRAPHIC CREDITS

ACKNOWLEDGEMENTS

I am most grateful to the writers of the works cited in the further reading, and particularly to Marian Campbell, Johann Michael Fritz and Ronald Lightbown for the opportunity of discussing medieval goldsmiths with them. I would also like to thank all those museum curators who have shown me their collections, and all those who have organised the remarkable series of medieval exhibitions listed in the further reading. For the British Museum photographs, I wish to express my gratitude to all the photographers, past and present, who have worked in the Department of Medieval and Later Antiquities. Within British Museum Press, Celia Clear has provided great encouragement for both the series and this particular book. Finally, I would like to thank Roger Davies for the design and Rachel Rogers for her good humoured and efficient editing.

INDEX